The Pragmatic Backpacker

Sensible Strategies for Savvy Backpacking

David Kunz

Cover photo by the author
East Fork Basin, Bridger Wilderness, Wyoming
Photography by Aaron Norton
Edited by Ashley S. Evans

Cover produced with Publisher Plus
Self-published with Amazon
Kindle Direct Publishing

To Keith, the Superman dad,
for walking me into the wilderness.

CONTENTS

ACKNOWLEDGMENTS

This project was entirely my wife's idea. Seeing that I was a reluctant writer, Holly challenged me to get my wilderness understanding out of my head and on paper. She also patiently managed the house and kids alone—regularly without any form of communication with me or knowledge of my whereabouts—while I wandered in a wilderness area states away. She knew she married someone who adores the outdoors but didn't sign up for this level of seasonal abandonment. Thank you, honey. I couldn't have done this without your encouragement.

Much gratitude goes to numerous hiking mentors and companions who were always game for adventure, but especially to Aaron, who has been the horse out of the gate for several hundred miles by my side. He consistently brought electrifying anticipation, an unselfish nature, and a listening ear.

Thank you to my resilient children, Allison, Cameron, Jared, and Sam, who were patient while Dad was gone but willing to jump into the journeys when they were old enough to tote a backpack.

And as much as I don't want to credit a global pandemic, it was within this new, slower coronavirus world and the endless event cancellations it caused that provided the abundant quiet hours essential for writing. Brighter days ahead.

CHAPTER 1
LOGICAL LESSONS

A few weeks before beginning middle school, I found my father in the garage arranging a rickety external-frame pack for me to safely survive in the woods. No, he wasn't kicking me out—a backpacking trip was planned for the upcoming weekend. I saw him using hooked bungee cords to clip on a military-surplus feather bag. He rolled up an extra pair of blue jeans in case my hiking pair got wet. I remember that the corners of my thick green poncho had brass grommets to double as a tarp. I was armed with all-leather boots, a nifty aluminum mess kit, a foam can of worms, a compass, and a promise. He said the lake was three-and-a-half miles in, seven miles roundtrip. My prepubescent brain couldn't fathom how far one mile was, let alone three and a half.

While we hiked, he slung a classic fabric-lined metal canteen across his sweaty chest. The canteen technology was primitive. If the outer cloth was kept wet, the inner metal and water were cooled, or at least that was the theory.

I was quick to sit on each inviting log along the trail for a break. He didn't join me. Instead, Dad stayed on his feet, bent one leg uphill, and planted his elbow on a knee, like a captain conquering a hill. I supposed it was his no-nonsense hack to avoid getting back up from sitting down while lugging a heavy pack. Gravity gave his shoulders a brief respite from the riveted canvas straps as he leaned forward. Sweat dripped from his nose, soaked his forehead, and formed a classic Superman hair curl. Between the brown curl, the rock jawline, and his broad shoulders, his likeness to Christopher Reeve was uncanny.

As we walked the trail, I'm sure I inquired how far we've gone every quarter mile. He'd give vague estimates to provide hope, but I'm sure he would've rather answered, "Not far enough. Keep walking."

He never called the mountains where we hiked the Uintas, always the *High* Uintas. The title gave the upper wilderness area an intimidating allure and esteem as their peaks looked down on the sprawling green forests and valleys of the lower range.

Once we arrived at the target lake, I helped assemble a green tent for the two of us. Then it was off to fishing, hoping for a red plastic bobber to dive deep below the surface under the pressure of a rainbow trout. My attention would rapidly get distracted from the focus required to stare at stillwater. After looking around and then back at the water, I would always hope to *not* see my bobber. Instead, I'd want it on the move or sunken.

"Got one!"

Rapid reeling would commence. Silent prayers were offered that the line wouldn't go limp.

On bitter mornings, Dad was the master of the griddle. The hand-size aluminum frying pan would heat unevenly, but he'd still produce a semi-browned pancake for breakfast complemented with a tiny syrup container. The cold air would stagger syrup viscosity. Once full, I would hand him a sticky pan and instantly head for the shore with a wriggling worm threaded on an Eagle Claw hook. I never appreciated how he would eat last and cover the clean-up—something I suppose most kids don't notice.

David and Keith summit Red Knob Pass (12,200 ft) in the High Uintas.

Religious returns to the same lake each July may just have been a father taking his son outdoors at the time, but with reflection, they sink deeper with purpose. The lasting value was witnessing Dad operate.

He was immaculately prepared for every event, whether it be a blown radiator hose or a wild trout needing prep for the fire. He would plan against a dead battery not only by packing jumper cables but by giving the engine one last throttle-charging rev before shut-off at the trailhead. He had small twine for tarp ties, backup forms of fire starters, mini plastic shakers for salt and pepper, and a foldable wood saw for firewood. I would carefully watch how he assembled each fishing pole and each hot meal. The outdoors was his primitive classroom of weather mindfulness, personal safety, and gear organization. Like the trout he helped me catch as his student-son, I was hooked for life.

Driven for Decades

Over thirty years of adolescence and adulthood, of college years and full-time jobs, I've managed to slowly log—literally log in a spreadsheet—thousands of miles on the vast public lands of the American backcountry. As many as possible were navigated off-trail and trekked above 10,000 feet. They required hundreds of nights sleeping in a tent after carefully selecting the right spot. This journal of journeys includes several short out-and-back overnight trips, but most marches were in the three- to seven-day range; the longest was an epic ten-day expedition.

Several adventurers have logged more miles in less time or spent weeks at a time racking up nights in their tent. But I separate myself from these summer-long hikers and lifestyle wanderers, as my approach has been steadily squeezing these miles in over weekends and weeklong treks while balancing the demands of raising a family, taking on new jobs in new states, and trying to live a balanced life with competing hobbies.

So much of backpacking instruction is imparted from the lens of professional guides or summer-long cross-continental explorers. Don't get me wrong—envy abounds for those who experience this free-range, oft-wandering lifestyle. Guiding as a profession isn't easy and highly coveted. Bucket lists abound of those who yearn to continually cover sections of the diverse Pacific Crest Trail, the eye-popping Continental Divide Trail, or the famous Appalachian Trail—or all three! These months-long journeys are remarkable and require years of preparation.

But the majority of backpackers approach the wild from their day job, from a weekend-warrior perspective. It's not their lifestyle. They are the 99%. Working professionals temporarily channel their inner wild person during short windows away from the grind and with limited budgets, without re-supply points. This guidebook is written for accountants who strive for adventures, supervisors who summon their inner survivalist, and teachers who become trip leaders.

Vacation days are a limited resource. Long weekends come but few times a year, and the high country only allows visitors to see its green slopes in mild weather a few months of the year. Combine this scarcity with competition from other hobbies, family commitments, or work conflicts, it makes every moment sweeter when a trip comes off without a hitch.

Despite not having a summer off nor a month at a time to disappear on extended cross-continental voyages, I've never let a year pass without a handful of carefully planned treks. Like countless working professionals, I've always operated within the finite limitations of paid time off, vacation days, annual leave—whatever your industry calls them. I plan two or three multi-day or weeklong adventures each summer. Scattered through the shoulder seasons, I draw up build-your-own long weekends as work and weather permit.

If this real-world, work-life restriction rings familiar, you may be in luck. This book is tailored to the average weekend warrior who has limited time off. When they do plan a full week in the woods, they want to make it count. They don't want to waste a day fumbling around with amateur-hour mistakes.

Why Pragmatic

Use this guidebook to stand on the proven practices and careful considerations of someone who has made the mistakes for you. Benefit from another who has wasted money on the wrong equipment or wasted time in the wrong direction. Use the strategies from someone who has explored ultralight backpacking extremes and backed it off a bit. Learn from another who has pushed daily mileage limits to see how it feels, then settled on more reasonable distances for reasons to be discussed.

Backpacking pragmatically embodies its definition by "dealing with things sensibly and realistically in a way that is based on practical rather than theoretical considerations." So much of exploring outdoors is conjured in theory with hours spent pouring over maps during winter blizzards, dreaming of warm afternoons among purple wildflowers in the months to follow. We strike a bet that a prescribed amount of preparation can get us from the trailhead to target in a certain number of days.

Whether solo or part of a group, the countdown to each trip approaches with Christmas-grade anticipation. Then, sadly, a few miles or days into the sticks, things change. Gear fails, legs tire, weather rumbles, groups disagree, elevation becomes more rugged than envisioned, and disappointing alterations are inevitable. Then the dreaded solution is voiced "Maybe we should hike out early."

After spending months preparing, weeks counting down, celebrating vacation days, and spending hundreds of dollars on gear to get deep in the outdoors, too many overwhelmed hikers can't plan early exits fast enough. Each time it's because they've encountered an unforeseen force of nature, tricky topography, or overestimated their feet or fortitude.

With experience, unexpected course adjustments—or cancellations—become nearly extinct. Sensibility sees through sensationalism. Pragmaticism affects every detail, including how much elevation can reasonably be tackled in a day. It addresses the practicality of how many hours are required to shuttle a group to a trailhead. Fact rises above fantasy. Hard-won intelligence keeps imagination in check.

The pragmatic backpacker also requires balance, a sense of the various Catch-22s that exist with wilderness decisions. Whether it's gear selection or campsite considerations, it's not wise to get sold on polarized extremes. Moderation is the key to unlock the right path through the trade-offs. You must become an expert—or counsel with experts—to reasonably weigh risks and benefits.

With housing, for example, you can choose either extreme. One can go ultralight with a minimal hammock that may swing sideways in a hailstorm or sweat each step while lugging a lunky double-wall tent that's twice what's needed between you and your buddy. There are risks and rewards for either extreme.

More Than You'll Need

Another reason for a more pragmatic approach is the seemingly endless selection of outdoor gear to sort through. Whether you're trying to update, lighten, or even begin your packing list, the average aspiring outdoor enthusiast is greeted with too many brands, categories, gadgets, and marketing messages to understand where to begin.

This vast selection confuses the hopeful with compelling appeals of weight, comfort, durability, breathability, cost, versatility, weatherproofing, and size. And that long list isn't comprehensive! Each brand and each model are marketed to scream out its strengths but hide its Achilles heel.

For example, would you like a backpack?

One popular outdoor retailer's website asks you to sort through 140 different packs to find "the one." And that's *after* filtering out daypacks and school backpacks. On a weeklong trip, my packing list totals about 37 pieces of gear and clothing items, not including small toiletry items. Contrast that with the thousands of apparel items and pieces of equipment each brick-and-mortar or online outlet is prepared to peddle. Approaching this onslaught requires realism and sensibility to filter it down to what few dozen items make the cut.

Not only is there an incredible quantity to sift, but there's a budget to balance. Backpacks aren't cheap. The majority of models are too expensive, complicated, heavy, feature-rich, or overly built for the average user. We just need something to carry our stuff a few miles in reasonable comfort. We're not summiting Denali.

A wide selection is not any retailer's fault, nor is it a bad thing. Let's celebrate so many options! But to navigate it pragmatically is a challenge.

Getting outside is a massive industry. According to the Outdoor Industry Association's recent report, recreation consumer spending exceeds $887 billion per year. This somehow outpaced dollars spent on pharmaceuticals and motor vehicles. Broken down further, they report that camping and trail sports, which encompass backpacking, made up more than $300 billion spent annually. $300 billion!

Recently I was excited to buy a shoe marketed to thru-hikers. The model promised mesh breathability and featherlight weight for long hauls. However, after one rugged 50-miler, the front hinge points of the mesh upper were blown out. The importance of breathable mesh disappointed in comparison to the durability of sturdier materials. This pragmatic backpacker was reminded of a gear truth: few materials can promise both breathability and durability. Choose one.

And it's not just gear. Several intangible decisions like campsite selection have trade-offs.

For example, desirable camping spots are rare in high-country irregular terrain. One well-used site may have flat ground for an obvious tent site; it may also have seen a summer of traffic. Your flat spot will come with the price of stamping your tent and gear on the dusty ground your whole stay, whereas a neighboring site may have a bit of slope but enough fresh groundcover to keep yourself and your gear clean coming in and out of the tent. I select the latter, as I prefer sloped cleanliness to flat dust.

Avoiding Extremes

At the risk of turning off some readers, I'd counsel you to guard yourself against a few backpacking extremes. I've conversed with enthusiasts who pride themselves on their platform. They preach one of these practices, and frankly, it gets old. Just as dogmatic extremists in politics or religion sours the enjoyable Thanksgiving table, don't stray too far down one of these paths. Not because any are inherently wrong—on the contrary, like politics and religion, they have value and can be quite inspiring and meaningful to followers. The pitfall is that the dogma too often becomes the *reason* to backpack and the obsessive sole topic of conversation.

There's an expression: "Hike your own hike." Even in writing this book, I have to guard against telling someone how to backpack, that somehow this pragmatic way is the best. Spoiler alert: it may not be. Instead, this book's purpose is to explore trade-offs and help others avoid pitfalls I've stumbled into, literally and figuratively. (I have scars to prove it!)

The following two ideologies are ones to sidestep. Watch for additional unproductive behaviors and attitudes in the sport you may encounter and choose to dismiss.

Beware the Macho Mileage Monster

"How many miles was it?"

This is by far the number one question I get asked when someone learns I went backpacking last week. I habitually take the bait and explain the route, then I remember why a handful ask: to compare my trip to a longer expedition they did one time—the old one-up. If it's not this usual conversation, it's hearing others brag about their death march in which the sole focus is on miles per day or total mileage. We get it. You walked really far.

The danger in this focus is that it tends to make someone second-guess if their "lesser" adventure was second-class; their 25-miler was inherently inferior to someone's 55-miler. And believe me, I've gone down the path of feeling menial and trying to be the mileage monster. I've punched several high-mileage outings. I've notched my belt on a 20-mile day with a full pack that included a 12,000-foot off-trail talus pass just to see if I could physically do it. And after all those trails and all those miles, I remember the most when I stop and turn around to appreciate where I've hiked, or when I sit on a stone and smell the wind.

Beyond my limited experience, there are several amateur and professional athletes—and I don't use the term *athletes* lightly—who blaze incredible distances and unimaginable time records as they cover entire states or cross-sections of continents. These are not macho mileage monsters; they are trained experts. The concern comes not from athletic achievement but when the focus of a trip report among average backpackers is mileage only. There is so much more to discuss and celebrate!

Let's strive to ask each other different questions. I suggest, "What was your favorite part?"

"What did you learn?"

"Did your gear work for you?"

"Would you do it again?"

There's certainly a time to put the hammer down and rack up the miles, and it's exhilarating to look back at the vast valley or distant ridge you were walking on just a few hours ago. But the pragmatic backpacker guards themselves from focusing too much on miles marched and more on miles *seen*.

Intentionally look past your next step on the trail, beyond the ankles of those hiking in front of you. The more you trek, the more you'll want to look around. Repeatedly on loop routes and thru-hikes, which we discuss later, the importance of taking mental and physical photos as you go is heightened as this may be your only moment on that part of the mountain, often for your whole life!

11

I regret not doing this enough. Don't make this mistake.

I once sketched out a 57-mile out-and-back to a distant drainage that promised excellent fishing and punishing vertical ups and downs along the way. Only a third was on a maintained trail. Our three-man group powered through it heads-down. We marched up switchbacks, nursed blisters, swapped gear, and forded glacial streams, all in what felt like a nervous hurry. Very few photos were snapped, and numerous vistas were neglected. Even our early exit felt hurried.

If I could do it again, I'd gear down, not to make it a more extended week, but to take a moment to scan the horizon, look at the clouds, or spot distant wildlife. The views were there—I saw them out of the corner of my tunnel vision—but I was focused on the next step and the map. As I think about it more, it's been enough years. Perhaps it's time for a redo.

Beware the Ultralight Gram-Counter

"How much does it weigh?" has become an everyday question in the sport. Whether it's your base pack weight or that titanium spoon, weight is tipping the scale of our intentions—pun intended. And for multitudes, being lighter is no longer a tool for success; it has become the entire endgame.

Pack weight used to be clocked in pounds the night before launch or a heft-at-trailhead guesstimate. That's it. Now grams are the standard when looking at the specs of each piece of gear. Sure, gram measurements outside of America are the standard. It makes sense. But now, pounds and ounces don't seem to have the small increment necessary—nor the minute marketing appeal—to accurately convey that this headlamp is really light. Like, 54 grams light!

Full disclosure: I am a huge proponent of going light. I've spent a decade moving my pack from the classic 45-pound beast of burden to my compact weeklong system in the mid-teens.

During this pound-shedding journey, I've noticed the emergence of *ultralight* as an overused backpacking buzzword. Beyond this boundary, *super-ultralight* has arisen as a newer, more-enticing marketing term used to attract gram-counters with pack base weights in single digits. There is no definition nor weight threshold to distinguish the two classifications, and they both profess themselves as the true way to backpack.

The pragmatic backpacker should focus on going *light* first. Worry about achieving so-called ultralight status later if desired but beware the enigmatic trade-offs.

Diminishing Return

I've quizzed a handful in the super-ultralight culture the following unanswerable question to showcase potentially wasted efforts encountered in the ideology: Where is the point of diminishing return?

A zealot could spare no expense, buy the lightest gear with the highest down rating, the finest titanium, and the thinnest nylon weave, then confidently tote just a handful of pounds. For many of these enthusiasts, their weeklong base weights are sub-ten pounds before adding food. That's incredible! This community is passionate about their practice and convinced they can hike further and more comfortably. Their days will be extended, their joints relieved.

But how does anyone truly know their eight-pound pack gives a physically distinguishable advantage over an 11-pound rig, or 13 for that matter?

At some point along that same trail, every hiker will eventually fatigue. Bones and muscles still tire even if bareback carrying zero pounds.

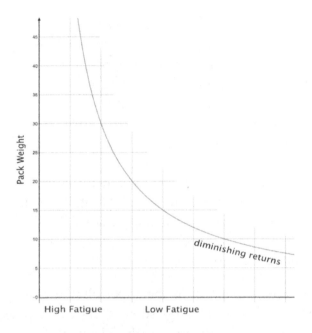

This unscientific illustration displays the dispute. Plotting base weight and fatigue, there's a convex downward-curved "benefit" line that drops considerably at first when shedding pounds from 45 to 20. At the apex of the curve, the benefit line loses angle into diminishing returns, losing *noticeable* benefit. Further across the graph, the line nearly flattens.

Yet disciples keep pushing, convinced an 11-pound pack is superior to one that's 14. Or that a single-digit pack is the ultimate. The ultralight theory argues the graph is a diagonal line, evermore beneficial with each ounce down to zero. Every sport has extreme edges.

Part of my caution may just be jealousy. I've tried several times to cut weight and get my already small base weight below ten pounds, but each time I encounter trade-offs of comfort, durability, or versatility that I'm not willing to compromise.

And then I ask myself, "What benefit am I seeking to gain?" Or "Will cutting another pound or two help me go farther or catch more fish?" The rhetorical answer is a resounding "not really."

Of course, it's different for each body type, male or female. At some unknowable point, spending and sacrificing to save those last few pounds or ounces does little-to-nothing to help. It becomes *only* sacrifice and expense, which is a net negative. No one knows where the point of diminishing return really lays.

I've settled into a base weight in the low teens (before food and water). It takes religious dedication to dive deeper into the ultralight or super-ultralight realm. Those who operate in single-digit-pack territory are dedicated experts of the craft and admirable for their innovation. However, my hope for this work is to inspire the weekend warrior and working professional, who may not have time to analyze grams, to experience lightweight backpacking off-the-shelf.

So, back off a little. Give yourself a break. Beware the gram-counting. Get yourself into as light of a pack as you pragmatically can. We will review some sensible and proven strategies. The benefits are indisputable and stark, moving from 40 to 20 pounds and further, but debatable after a certain point. Keep your eyes on the prize more than the scales. The award is how you *feel* out there.

Are you colder than you'd like?

Are you well-rested on the right pad?

Are you still hungry after a hard day's hike?

Are you dry after the deluge?

And most importantly, are you safe?

If you're always cold at night because your ultralight sleep system isn't cutting the chill, your micro pack weight is no longer beneficial. Likewise, if you're wet from minimal rain gear, your ultralight pack isn't going to help dry you off. Be smart and sensible out there.

Yes, a pragmatic approach to backpacking sounds a little boring. Think less tedious and more "I'd like to avoid wasting time on my vacation and wasting money on non-essential gear." Unless your idea of "exciting" is rerouting a weeklong trip midweek after not reasonably budgeting mileage or overloading your first day, a common mistake of the overly optimistic covered later. Savvy backpacking starts with a modest mindset and a simplified setup but includes much more.

Make the most of each precious day off when walking away from your routine with everything you need—and less of what you don't—strategically strapped to your back. As you do, you'll experience a more pragmatic approach to backpacking. You'll be more apt to dispatch the focus given to the dizzying selection of products, brands, gadgets, and destinations. You'll instead encounter the outdoors simply and sensibly, based on real-world practices. Stripped away from misconceptions and consumer clutter, your goal of the steep summit, the distant lake, or the pink sunrise will become more realistic and achievable.

CHAPTER 2
NOW MORE THAN EVER

Why backpacking? Why not just go car camping, RVing, or something simpler? Backpacking seems so involved and tedious. The answer: now more than ever, we as a species need to be backpacking. There are three primary reasons the sport should be prioritized against various competing recreational activities: the great indoors, the advancements in off-road vehicles, and a generational need to do hard things.

The Overwhelming Draw of the Great Indoors

Never in the history of humankind has the draw of modern convenience experienced in the comfort of home been so compelling and addictive. At the tap of a screen, anything can be delivered from a new car to fresh groceries. Disney's *Wall-E* nailed the tale foretelling elements of this era—lazy, screen-addicted citizens who seem ever-more relatable each year.

In addition, the need to commute is becoming rarer, especially after 2020 pandemic conditions. Working from home has never been a more prevalent option for so many positions and professions. The need to step outside has never been so low, and yet, so high. I'm not a psychologist nor an anthropologist, but I suspect there will be years of studies done on those living in this period to assess the damaging effects of opting out of hours previously spent outdoors.

For the past few hundred years, humans have striven to create increasingly more favorable indoor environments to lessen the stress of battling the elements. I fear the pendulum has swung too far. I love automatic air conditioning and doorstep deliveries as much as the next guy, but there needs to be a deliberate and consistent effort to complement these hours saved with days dealing with wind, navigating a forest, wandering a trail, or peering over water. Spending time outside helps us gain a grateful perspective on how far we've come. Being outdoors improves mental health, stimulates physical conditioning, and will better your soul through an endless list of psychological, emotional, physiological, and medical benefits.

In the early 90s, I found a summer job working as a whitewater river guide. My work was to help youth and adults experience the outdoors in a way rarely taught today—bouncing down a river in an old-fashioned 15-foot aluminum canoe. While directing them to navigate currents, side channels, and obstacles, I would ponder on where they would ever need to deploy these skills again. No sporting goods stores sold these silver canoes. They sold plastic kayaks and more skin-friendly fiberglass canoes. And even if they bought a canoe, when would they bounce through rapids ever again?

Likely never, but that wasn't the point.

The purpose was to give youth who spend most of their lives indoors at school or home an outdoor experience of a lifetime—rarely, if ever, to be repeated. The combination of moving water, bald eagles around every bend, obstacle evasion, and burning sunshine would create permanent memories. Youth and parents would approach me at the end of excursions, still wearing their orange PFDs, look me in the eye, and express their deep gratitude with a wet handshake. Some were brought to tears. I give credit to the allure of moving water under big skies.

When freed from the indoor confines of sheetrock homes and concrete cities, the outdoors teaches us how small we are compared to its power. The elements elevate our thoughts to gratitude for the comfort and safety we so readily enjoy.

The Overwhelming Ability of Off-Road Vehicles

Vehicles once primarily used for agriculture or hunting—turning water, managing fences, or removing game—are now entire recreational industries themselves. Four-wheelers and ATVs have evolved into side-by-side UTVs with crew-cab seating and advanced suspension systems. Where trucks used to be unable to pass, these off-road vehicles thrive and thrill.

As a result, in the past decade, we've seen an unfortunate and marked increase in dirt scars on steep hillsides, increased use of previously abandoned forest roads, and new roadside play trails carved wherever public access can be obtained. Impassible terrain used to limit the average high-clearance truck or Jeep, but it seems only locked gates and national forest wilderness area boundaries are the new limits. And sometimes, even those are disregarded.

I learned to study these boundaries more closely after designing a 60-mile circular route in the northern end of my favorite range. Midweek is when I expect to be the most remote during a trek. The farther you explore from the trailhead, the fewer folks you typically see. Day three found me rounding the upper corner of the circuit. Rumors of good fishing at the back of one cirque drew me in. I wanted to see it for myself.

Arriving at the high lake, I noticed it backs against the Continental Divide at nearly 11,000 feet. I was surprised to spy a few yellow dome tents lined along the distant shoreline. Then I noticed a well-worn trail on the opposite slope dropping down from the horizon saddle. Silhouetted on the far ridgeline were three red UTVs. Here I was, on foot after thirty miles like an idiot in what I thought was a remote area, but vehicles had made it in as well.

Once home, I discovered this particular saddle not only hosted the Continental Divide but also the Fitzpatrick Wilderness Area boundary. Motorized vehicles were legal all the way to the ridge where they had parked. Measuring their ride showed 45 miles of dirt road plus an additional 10 miles of near-impossible terrain for even the toughest of trucks. But these machines made it look easy and put their drivers within a few hundred yards of a mountain-top lake with an endless view.

I'm not against these vehicles when used correctly and legally. They are a blast! And for many, they are the only option to access the outdoors. But they add pressure to the backcountry in numbers never before seen, causing solitude—and quiet—to be a more sought-after and scarce resource.

Enter backpacking.

The Bridger Wilderness offers unmatched vistas for those willing to walk.

Walk away from common car camping spots inundated with motorized gadgets. Placing even one or two miles between your next camping spot and the gate which keeps out a motor vehicle changes the outdoors from a popular playground to a quiet personal corner of paradise. Quick solitude awaits when you follow a path into a roadless area, beyond a gated trailhead, or into a remote part of the 110 million acres of federally protected wilderness area.

The Underwhelming Challenge of Car Camping

You pull up to the campground and unload the car. There's a fire pit, a picnic table, a tent site, and maybe a covered shelter. Yes, you'll be sleeping in a tent, but perhaps not technically on the ground. Your vehicle could carry a cot, a big air mattress, or even tow a beige RV—all good options to keep your sleep more like home.

If the wind whips up and it starts to rain, you can duck into the truck and watch the wild storm pass through a windshield—which is literally called a wind shield! If you get cold, you can warm up in the car or camper with electric heat powered by a generator. If you forget something, you can run a quick errand to a nearby town. There are collapsible lawn chairs for furniture, hose spigots for culinary water, picnic tables for mealtime, and shared bathrooms.

Nearly every outdoor obstacle that could be encountered, save it be the dirt on the ground (wait, there are concrete pads and rugs for that!) can be solved with the campground amenities, the vehicles, or the bulky belongings they can carry. How wonderful! And yet, how underwhelming.

One might ask, "Why did you even go camping?" "Why didn't you just stay home?" "What did you hope to experience?"

Again, car camping and "glamping" have their place in the outdoors. It's straightforward and approachable. It's a getaway for millions. Like using off-road UTVs, car camping is frequently the only way some can safely experience the outdoors. But in our never-ending quest to mitigate every inconvenience of the elements, we weaken something primal that's hard-wired in our DNA: resilience.

The more advanced we become at mitigating outdoor elements, obstacles, and adversity, not only do we lessen the chances of *encountering* trouble, but we weaken our *ability* to overcome it. That's resilience lost. It's the toughness that tells us, "I've been through worse. I can handle this."

The simple act of finishing my first seven-mile-roundtrip trek with my dad provided a resilience framework for years. If something was a mile away in town, I knew I had hiked farther. I knew it was about a half-hour of walking. If a storm erupted and I wasn't indoors, I learned how to find the right tree to duck under to stay the driest and wait for it to pass. I've seen worse. I've done hard things before. That's resilience in action.

Part of the mission of the U.S. Marine Corps is to train marines to adapt, overcome, and improvise their way through any obstacle or situation. We can't all be marines, but we can create intentional outdoor experiences that help us naturally build long-lasting resilience.

"Oorah!"

The remaining chapters provide how-tos and hacks for your next resilience-required outing. Your pack will get lighter, plus you'll gain gear acumen, route-plotting know-how, boots-on-the-ground wisdom, and be better prepared to select provident foods, superior campsites, and well-matched partners.

CHAPTER 3
GOING LIGHT SOLVES PROBLEMS

Years ago, I found myself training a youth group on backpacking. As the guest instructor, I asked all to rattle off the reasons people don't enjoy backpacking. We wrote the predictable answers on the slippery dry erase board: blisters, back pain, sweaty miles, bulky packs, injury, it takes forever. I was delighted at the spot-on answers as they set up a perfect discussion on how going light can solve all six complaints. This small-sample survey speaks volumes for the masses. The focus group nailed it for all interested in the sport but leery of its drawbacks and physical price tag. Still, others hope that perception persists as it removes the cautionary and concerned from the backcountry, thereby increases space for those already in-the-know.

But what if there was a method for removing nearly every concern with one adjustment? It would be a kill-six-birds-with-one-stone fix.

Going light solves problems, period. In fact, it almost solves every major frustration encountered by both the novice and the more experienced who want to do more in the sport but have reservations or physical limitations. Lighter gear supports proper posture, enhances mobility, diminishes difficulty, lengthens distances, increases speed, promotes safety, reduces risks, decreases sore spots, and eliminates blisters.

Counting Calories

Imagine if you were asked to write down every item you ate and its calorie count for one day; this is a standard weight-loss strategy.

Would you eat more or less that day? My money's on the latter.

As calories are measured, they're questioned. This vigilant diet logic not only works on waistlines, it works on packs. Start "watching your diet" by measuring what you're currently "eating." As each piece of equipment seeks entry into your collection, it needs to be weighed down to the ounce, the tenth of the ounce, or gram. Just as full-sized meals and small snack calories are calculated, so too are tents and toothpaste.

Pen, paper, spreadsheet, or back of a napkin, I don't care about your method—just get your gear assessed and be thorough. Don't allow items to slip into pack pockets unchecked.

It's hard to weigh a t-shirt on a bathroom scale, so you'll need an inexpensive postal or food scale like those found for $15-20 online. If your workplace uses postage, there may be a digital scale in the building. I've been known to stay late after closing, balancing tents stakes and titanium sporks on a corporate postal scale that gives readings to the tenth of the ounce. Heavier gear can be weighed in comparison to your weight on a digital bathroom scale. It's not perfect, but it's close enough to compare lighter options.

Once your gear is measured, it will tell its own story. The sore thumbs will stick out. You'll immediately see what "high-calorie" items need to be rejected and reconsidered. This is the first step in an eye-opening journey to lighten your load. You'll discover that shirts weigh half a pound. Nalgene bottles are surprisingly heavy compared to hydration bladders. Warm jackets, if not down or thin nylon, can be one of your heaviest items. The goal is to get you to hesitate when reaching for that extra shirt or a fourth pair of wool socks.

Don't dismiss an item because it's only a few ounces. Remember: two nickels make a dime. Start behaving as selectively as someone looking in the fridge late at night with the looming goal to lose ten pounds before swimsuit season. Let's explore sensible strategies to lessen and lighten your gear.

Less is More

Going lightweight is more than minimalism—a helpful mindset, but not the end. Don't be a minimalist just to carry less stuff. Think minimally to increase the time doing something *other* than managing your gear while unpacking, setting up, taking down, organizing, packing, or rifling through your pack along the trail for something you need. Less stuff equals more reasons you planned this trip! Every item you bring, no matter how small, has to be managed. Every minute spent sorting through your gear or moving one widget from here to there is one not spent *backpacking*—you're not looking around, casting a line, listening to the wind, or getting lost gazing at the scale of the distant slope.

Instead, you're carrying and creating a chaotic situation that requires more tedious management.

When my kids were little, I noticed our small condo stayed cleaner not only when we had fewer toys but when the tiny tots chose to play with the singular toys that day rather than the sets. At the end of the day, I'd pick up a few toys, and the house was done. However, when the Legos were remembered, or the puzzles, much more pick-up ensued after bedtime. Knowing this pet peeve of mine, my father-in-law, Bruce, purposely bought my small daughter a 64-piece kitchen cooking playset complete with plastic green celery and other groceries, tiny pink pots, little lids, and so forth. When she tore off the wrapping paper, she was thrilled. He saw my horror and started to belly laugh. It was half gift for her and half prank for me.

Recently I was packing up my campsite on the second day of a weeklong journey. I was almost done putting away my tent but couldn't find the little orange stuff sack where the seven stakes are supposed to be stored. I eventually found it a few feet away, blown into some dried wildflower stems, when it hit me.

Why am I allowing this empty bag to cause me a chore all week?

Why not just use a rubber band wrapped on one stake, or simply keep the stakes tucked on the side of the tent's stuff sack? The miniature bag didn't add measurable weight, but it added work. It was one more thing to manage, monitor, or fear losing at each campsite.

Pragmatic backpacking questions each item. Have a strict nagging voice on one shoulder pestering you if the trial-size deodorant is essential. Too often, to the demise of well-intentioned packers, the pack-rat character sitting on the opposite shoulder is whispering, "But you might *need* it."

Don't listen!

Ask yourself these types of questions: Do I need all of these shirts? Does each serve a single purpose, or can each be used in two or more situations?

Single-purpose items need to be put on trial and questioned on the witness stand for their lack of versatility. I used to cart a nylon swimsuit for a mid-week dip in a frigid lake. This optional occasion is a refreshing trip highlight. But that one piece of clothing, even if rolled tight, had to be packed and unpacked a dozen times during a weeklong trek as apparel is sorted in and out of the tent daily. It would get buried at the bottom of the pack, taking up space and adding extra ounces, awaiting its one moment all week—a minutes-long plunge. The solution was simple—skip the suit. Everyone I journey with wouldn't be offended seeing a brief bare backside or a dive in compression underwear. Besides, swimming in clothing is a clever tactic to tackle laundry.

Dual-use apparel is more desirable. I have a long-sleeved breathable fishing shirt that doubles as a bugproof layer during breezy days, especially when my regular hiking shirt starts to stink toward the end of the week.

The only cotton item I tote is a red handkerchief. What's its purpose? Of course, a forehead sweat rag, but it's also a thin shammy for drying off wet limbs after a chilling dip in a lake. When wet, it's a left-handed grip for hanging onto the otherwise-slippery tail shank of a mature trout as I rarely carry a net. Tucked under a hat brim, it becomes sunshade to darken my eyes for an afternoon power nap.

Not only are daily clutter, chores, and checklists at stake with a longer gear list, so is weight—one of the critical considerations for each item.

Lighter Gear May Not Require Heavier Costs

One complaint of moving toward lightweight gear is the cost

of switching. This can be argued both ways. Several lightweight gear items cost the same or less than their heavier counterpart. Lighter backpacks, hooded rain jackets, apparel items, and some tents are less expensive due to their simplistic design (however, in the case of down sleeping bags, I'll concede that lighter bags will cost more than affordable synthetic-fill bags). And lightweight gear drives innovation toward cheap DIY alternatives. Tyvek ground cloths can replace fancy tent footprints, as discussed later. Two-dollar sports drink plastic bottles are lightweight and work just as hard as $15 name-brand bottles.

To take the sting out of the next upgrade's price tag, subsidize the switch by selling used gear. When properly cared for, quality gear holds value and has a market.

Five years ago, my only daughter could have pushed me over with a feather when she declared her interest in going on the annual pilgrimage to the Wind River Range in Wyoming. My fatherly excitement couldn't be contained. I spent months assembling every piece of gear necessary to make her first trek a success. Each month we prepared, I feared she would change her mind. But she never did. She was determined.

Part of the gear list was her own women's Osprey pack in a feminine teal color. When it was found on sale for $99 instead of $199, I pounced on the deal. She rocked that week—never complained once. She mastered packing her gear each morning with military-grade discipline. And she blessed me again the next year by returning for another adventure. Those two summers get me a little choked up if I allow myself to ponder them. The moral of the story is to never let your only daughter grow up.

But I digress.

The lesson at hand is that same women's pack was recently sold in the local classifieds for $80 cash to a college student interested in starting the sport. It was underused and retained its value. The new buyer was thrilled with the cute color and bounced off to her car. As I held the cash and watched her drive off, I smiled, recalling the memories the pack provided and realized the net cost was only $19—best deal ever!

Allison navigating off-trail in rugged granite terrain.

Another tip: avoid buying this year's model at full retail. Last year's tent and pack is a magnificent design at a fraction of the cost. Between reselling your heavy gear for cash and selecting last year's clearance stock, your gear conversion concerns can be minimized, limited budgets can be maximized.

There were a few years when my packing list was undergoing significant remodeling. After weighing each piece, I'd search out the smarter and lighter replacement. My ultralight backpacking mentor, Kent, and I came up with a fun measuring metric called "dollars per ounce." We were both operating on limited family budgets, and unfortunately, the best high-quality gear was frequently the most expensive. Good gear generally follows the mantra "buy once, cry once." With that in mind and careful consideration, we acquired selected pieces with a high dollars-spent-to-ounces-saved ratio.

"This $220 down jacket will save me eight ounces! That's $27 per ounce! Is that good?"

Despite our best efforts to justify expenditures, Kent and I never did arrive on what ratio was officially cost-effective, as "cost per ounce" was mostly in jest. But it helped us view gear costs through a different and more pragmatic lens.

I Remember Blisters

One mile into the trail and I can still hear Dad on high-alert hot-spot watch.

"Any hot spots?"

He would rarely call them blisters, but *hot spots*, slowly teaching me what the problem *feels* like. It's a spot on your foot that feels hot—simple enough. To this day, when I ask my sons the same, I catch myself sounding like Dad.

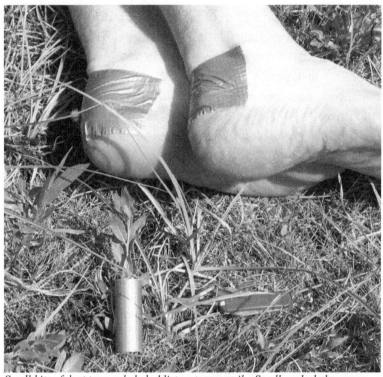

Small bits of duct tape only help blisters temporarily. Small packs help more.

For several years into backpacking on my own as a big boy, I would get a soggy first-day blister. As my base weight dropped into the twenties and then into the low teens, they vanished. I've since stopped worrying about them. I don't think I've had a blister in eight years or more. The outdoor brands that engineer boots and hiking shoes are getting more adept. Materials and construction are advancing to mitigate the three blister-causing elements: friction, heat, and moisture. Socks are becoming more advanced both in fabric and weave. But even with the best boots and the latest socks, lugging too much weight will create too much heat, friction, and moisture for the skin to handle.

Lightening your gear lessens the *friction* of each footstep and reduces *heat* as fewer calories are burned, which minimizes sweaty *moisture*. A lighter pack may feel great on your back and muscles, but your feet are direct beneficiaries—among the first of many.

Backpacking and blisters have been known to go hand-in-hand for decades. But light packs break the generational stereotype. Well-fitting footwear and quality socks help plenty, but nothing can compare to the relief found from half the pounds.

Backbreaker

If getting your pack strapped on requires another pair of hands or can't be done without placing the fabric monster on a boulder and then sitting down to wriggle into it, you've got some work to do. If you find yourself diving for a place to unclip from your back's beast of burden every time the group stops for a break, you're not going to have a good time.

I have unsightly photos from 15 years ago of myself and my brother-in-law, Aaron, along the trail, both towered by our back monsters. We had no idea there was a better way.

Well, that's not true.

We knew, but we were too confident, too broke, and too dismissive of the process to analyze and carefully convert all of our gear. Our friend, Kent, had been realizing the benefits of light gear for years. He taught us so much while comfortably toting what looked like half a pack. I'm sure his back winced a few times when learning what we brought along. I'm grateful for the wise mentors and safe soundboards I've hiked hundreds of miles alongside.

Your back, shoulders, and hips are the biggest beneficiaries of a lighter set-up. In fact, your whole skeleton will thank you. An entertaining side benefit of small and lightweight packs is the confused reaction from those you pass along the trail, generally when encountered a couple of days from the nearest trailhead. You can see the calculus processing in their head.

It generates concerned questions like, "Did you day hike here?" "Are you eating off the land?" "So, all your food is in there too?" "Do you have a tent?"

All are actual questions I've been asked. While visiting with the concerned, I notice I'm answering the interview with my skeleton standing up straight, shoulders back, and the top of my pack is below my collar. I feel great! On the other hand, they look miserable. Well, that's not fair. They look to be having a good trip but sore enough to avoid another weeklong march soon. Been there.

When your pack gets lighter, your back problems get solved quickly, thereby removing the number one fear and criticism of backpacking. Your body lasts longer. You can punch further into the forest. And do it again the next day. Spontaneous side trips and add-on options become more achievable.

Want to make it to that next lake before dinner? You've got this.

The Sweaty Face

Although not the biggest obstacle to backpacking, it's still an annoying irritant. Your shirt gets glued to your back, your forehead is runny, your hair gets crusty, and you've only gone two miles. When you lighten your pack, you'll never sweat again! Ok, that may or may not be true, but it certainly decreases the greases. Another indirect benefit is your hiking outfit lasts longer without the need for daily laundry. I still like to do a lakeside load of sweaty shirts and socks, but it's nice not to have to do it daily.

Better Than Bulky

A natural side effect of lighter gear is smaller stuff. Down jackets and bags compress to impress. Modern tent bags are tiny. And with more lightweight gear, backpack capacity requirements lessen, thereby lightening the pack itself. When the total pack size is narrower, natural arm swing improves, helping you stride down the red line on your map. When the pack isn't stacked above one's head, neck strain is reduced removing the need to hunch over. Neck mobility is increased, allowing you to birdwatch or eye the approaching storm. More weight can be comfortably placed on the hips, where it should be. Then your shoulder straps not only become secondary, but they start helping—as opposed to hanging—on your posture.

Small packs ride *with* you instead of *over* you. Your movements through rocky terrain or off-trail aren't jolted by a separate entity sloshing rhythmically off-beat and one step behind your stride. Bushwhacking through brush is a hassle. Short packs remove the concern to duck deep under branches without the extra bundle lurking above your skull. Lunging a faithful leap over a muddy mire or creek isn't burdened backward.

After enough miles of walking in sync and having it supply you with water and resources, a light pack feels like a part of you. It feels good to take it off, but you also feel a little naked without it. If you ever catch yourself have this feeling, you're doing it right.

Injury Reduction

Years ago, I was driving into the lane at a pick-up basketball game. The shot went up, but as I came down, a giant defender awkwardly fell on my back. The impact sent a concussion wave down my body, starting at my right shoulder and ending by crushing my right ankle. It would have been a wicked strain regardless, but having his weight and momentum added to my already large frame did twice the trauma. I was out for weeks watching the contusion change colors daily like a slow sunset from purple to green to orange. I've turned that ankle before, but never while wearing a 220-pound man-pack.

The same danger applies to heavy rigs. Ankles will sprain under natural body weight and inertia, but carrying weight amplifies damage. Going lightweight isn't just about comfort, posture, or bragging rights—it's about safety. Imagine walking down a flight of stairs carrying a 40-pound bag of flour. What would happen with a misstep?

This is every step over rocky and rooted terrain with your 45-pound pack. Each negative consequence is compounded. Reduce your risk. Give your ankle a chance to bounce back if you make a misstep. It'll happen. Give your knees half the damage if they get torqued. Not only is injury reduced, but your body's natural instincts have a fighting chance to react. Whether it's getting your hand down first or shifting to take the weight off the crumpling ankle right as you sense it buckling—it's intuitive. And it's helped without as much heaviness.

Despite injury, do it to give your joints half the strain each step. Weight-induced damage isn't limited to jolting contusions or sprains but can come by slight tears in tendons or hip-belt-friction bruises. These go unnoticed all day but greet you in the morning with a stretch or sore spot.

Good Gear Goes the Distance

"Backpacking is so slow." This complaint is especially valid when a group has one of four elements: beginners, the out-of-shape, heavy packs, steep terrain, or—heaven forbid—all four at once. This four-part combination is a recipe for mountain misery. Plan a slow or short day if this sounds like your group.

You cannot resolve all four circumstances on the trail, but plump packs can be shaken down weeks prior, and pre-trip practice hikes can pump up the learner's legs. Getting lighter gear gives the nervous novice the confidence to come again next year. It invigorates energetic youth with their smaller stride to the front of the pack train. It makes switchbacks up steep terrain feel like cardio instead of cardiac arrest for those not in the best shape.

I'm not an advocate for barreling down the trail at as high of pace as possible. On the contrary, I recommend enjoying the journey and taking breaks. But reasonable distances still need to be covered. Going light adds a go-the-distance advantage to hikers who embark into the hills without ideal bodies or vast experience.

My boys aren't allowed on weeklong 40- and 50-milers until they turn twelve. It's an arbitrary family rule, but it's worked thus far. Giving their boney bodies a little extra time to fill out adds to their safety and enjoyment for their big first journey. Until then, they practice on shorter five- and ten-milers. You'll come up with your own comfort levels for age and distances. Credit for these initial treks also lies in their lighter packs—and a pocket full of hard candy to keep teenage spirits high along with blood-sugar levels. Watching them start their week struggling with less than twenty pounds gets less stressful as they slowly acclimate to the altitude and eat down their consumable weight each day. A 100-pound 12-year-old carrying a 20-pound pack is going to struggle considering that's 20% of their body weight. Few adults would be comfortable with equivalent ratios. By week's end, their pack settles in the low teens. Confidence soars as they charge ahead of the group up rocky passes over 11,000 feet and wait for others at the windy top.

There's a high to be had when thighs are pumping up a peak with confidence: goosebumps, endorphins, and second winds kick-in. With a breeze chilling your back and under the reasonable weight of a thoughtfully prepared pack, you'll start to look forward to conquering contour lines. The miles start running together, and before long, you'll catch yourself saying, "Look, there's the lake. We're already here."

CHAPTER 4
THE BIG THREE

For decades, a cotton bedroll and a canvas tarp were about all outdoorsmen carried, whether afoot or on horseback. Then personal tents came along, mirroring what military groups used. The two-pole pup tent was a simple A-frame staple for a generation. Then double-wall tents arrived on the scene in the early 1980s, replacing single-layer canvas and nylon predecessors. They dominate the market today as the standard balance between climate control and ease of use. It's fascinating to watch how each generation of gear stands on the shoulders—and eventually replaces—the previous as trade-offs are addressed and downsides are eliminated.

Tents are one of "the big three," as called in the sport. Comprised of your shelter, your sleep system (bag and pad), and your pack. They are the three heaviest, the three bulkiest, and the three most expensive items. They require some consideration to avoid unnecessary weight and expense. Once refined, your carefully selected big three can swing your pack weight and size dramatically and give your "weight loss" goals a big head start.

Ruling Out Hammocks

I'm regularly asked why I don't use a hammock. Paired with a rainfly, they are functional for many. Each year, advances in their design make them a more comfortable and lightweight alternative to a tent. However, there are three reasons I don't use them: trees, spines, and elements.

Number one: I'm rarely camping where two trees are close enough to hang a hammock. When I lived in the Pacific Northwest for nine years, this was not the case. Nearly every night, one could count on a sturdy hemlock or cedar tree to be in the perfect spot. The thick hardwood forests of the American Midwest and Appalachian range offer similar structure. But the arid conifer forests of the alpine Rocky Mountain high country where I grew up and am living now are a whole different ecosystem. Rain is sparse, and trees grow spread apart to compete for root real estate. I frequently camp near or at the tree line (about 10,700 ft), where trees become sparse and stunted. If not too high, I'm regularly too low and camping in an arid, juniper-dotted river canyon bottom. So, hammocks are out. Also, sometimes I want the spot with the epic vista at sunrise, or I want to sleep with a lake view. Hammock users are limited to fewer options. They must have a spot with two sturdy trees, just the right distance from each other.

Second, I'm a side-sleeper. Hammocks are great for back-sleepers. If you want to curl with the fabric, like sinking into a plush armchair at home, then hammock away. But I haven't spent a night in a hammock where I woke up without spine issues.

The last deal-breaker for me, and arguably the most important, is the elements. The protection a double-wall system offers from wind, rain, frosty mornings, dew, mosquitos, and critters large and small can't be matched. I don't want to just be okay or "make it through" the night. I need to sleep and sleep deeply. I need to recover so I can push into new places the following day. I like to sleep as warm, as flat, and as protected as possible with earplugs cutting out distractions and ibuprofen soaking my sore muscles. Summer sunrises come earlier than I prefer. Tent walls give me that extra hour or two of procrastinating consciousness if I feel my body needs it.

If you can accomplish a successful and restful night's sleep in a hammock, go for it. You may save some weight and costs; however, one could argue that a hammock, paired with quality straps, hardware, and a rainfly offers only nominal weight savings to modern lightweight solo tents, which can be found under two pounds. In groups, the weight argument fails further as two hikers can split carrying a cozy "two-plus" or three-man tent that spreads the 35-45 ounces between them.

Back in the Tent

Bless you, outdoor product designers! Your innovations have made giant leaps in recent decades and significant improvements in recent years. The list of modern enhancements includes ripstop nylon, thinner-denier fabrics with less compromise, silicon-infused silnylon, taped seams, bathtub floors, mosquito netting flexibility, waterproofing improvements, reflective cordage with less bulk, quick-clip assembly, and minimized zippers for weight savings. And that's only a portion of what's been developed to lighten tents, improve their comfort, and increase weather resistance. Like new cars, it's difficult to buy a backpacking tent these days and not be impressed with its engineering.

Buy One Size Up

Solo tents are available for independent adventurers. Whether tenting on your own as part of a group or going solo, it seems only natural to only buy what you need. Minimalism is good.

One person only needs a one-person tent, right?

I've gone down this route and stopped. Solo tents are fine, but the biggest downside is the width-to-weight ratio. It isn't efficient. I feel like I'm being confined to a coffin.

The top five solo tents on the market today average 35" wide and typically taper toward the leg. If you want to feel snug or are a smaller-framed person, you might love it. I'm broad-shouldered and 75" tall. For only a few ounces more, I enjoy a two-man tent when solo. The same logic applies to camping with a buddy; buy one size up to the three-man tent. You'll thank me. You can toss some clothes around, have more room to change, and if the weather gets ridiculous, your pack can get an upgrade from vestibule to footsy on the tent floor.

The only times I've been comfortable sleeping two people in a two-man tent, and I've spoken with many who agree, is if your partner is your actual partner or your child. Cuddling is nearly unavoidable. Great for family, but friends—not so much. I'm willing to divide up the extra eight to ten ounces it takes to tote a three-man tent instead when hiking with a buddy. I'd rather not be shoulder-to-shoulder, especially after a few days when bodies start to get a little ripe. Two friends sharing a two-man tent also creates the awkward possibility of ending up face-to-face when turning over during the night or feeling like one of you needs to always be facing away. A lightweight three-man tent, or *two-plus* as some are categorized, is the ultimate sensible two-friends-and-some-gear home. It's also perfect for two plus a dog.

Waiting out an afternoon downpour surrounded by disheveled gear

Remember, regardless of the tent's size, you need to be able to do more than sleep. Don't say to yourself, "All I need is a place to sleep at night." Be realistic. Be prepared to live inside this little fabric frame for a few hours wide awake and see how that feels. Nearly every weeklong journey in the high country, I'm pinned into my nylon dome home during an afternoon deluge. If solo, I keep busy with a journal, a book, phone photo editing, or a study of the upcoming topo maps. With a buddy, we play cards or make each other laugh. All of this is difficult to do if your shoulders are touching the tent wall or your companion. By now, you can likely guess my feelings on bivy sacks.

Consider a few field-tested considerations to make in your next tent purchase. Look for tents with side entry rather than front. Doors at the head of the tent are tricky to enter and exit. Side doors are a must-have. Look at the spec sheet and consider peak height (for sitting up), length if long-legged, and weight. Save your budget and skip this year's latest release. Look for clearance models from previous years as new models get modest adjustments.

There are several great tentmakers, but Big Agnes consistently delivers some of the lightest designs with thoughtful engineering. Competition in the marketplace creates more options for reasonably priced lightweight tents that used to be reserved only for high-end spenders. Take good care of it, and your shelter can last years.

Footprints are for Suckers

No matter the tent, they've always come with extra caution: don't forget the ground cloth. Manufacturers don't call them tarps anymore; they are footprints—a perfectly matched piece of high-denier fabric, custom-built to protect the floor of your tent from moisture and abrasive damage. They are— luckily—sold separately. Don't buy them. They are expensive, heavy, and over-engineered. Several are about a half-pound of fabric and cost $35-70 extra.

Instead, do some DIY and buy Tyvek, a synthetic material that's impossibly lightweight, durable, breathable, and water-resistant. It's the same stuff houses are wrapped in during construction to allow the house to "breathe" in one direction while protecting it from moisture entering the other. It can be bought by the yard online in squares or tent-sized pieces for a fraction of the cost of a footprint. Then you can cut it to the exact shape of your tent floor.

Tyvek also saves you the grief when you're packing up and realize you slept on some pine pitch and gummed up the bottom of the material. Replace it in a few years without cost stress. Another footprint alternative is a clear painters' tarp from any hardware store. It comes in a few thicknesses and is inexpensive and waterproof. Durability is a little low but easily replaced when worn.

When custom-cutting your homemade tarp, regardless of the material, slice it just inside the outer edge of your tent's floor—no larger. Tarp exposed from under the tent during rain quickly becomes counterproductive by ushering the water that drips off the tent to directly under you. The rain that runs off your tent body should touch the dirt. As you crumple and stuff your ground cloth with your tent's stuff sack over and over, it will never fully flatten again, making for slightly smaller coverage by an inch or so around the whole edge. This is perfect; right where you want it.

Don't Be the Sleep-Under-The-Stars Hero

"Should we put on the rainfly?"

The question seems to come up every time I pitch a tent with someone. Rainflies carry the stigma that you're somehow wimping out. It's a warm afternoon, and covering a tent seems needless at such a hot time of day.

The answer: Yes.

Clear skies? Yes.

But it hasn't rained for days. Still, yes.

If you want to see the stars, stay up late, and lay on the ground. Alpine stargazing is unmatched!

Pro tip: if you're an astronomer at heart or want mind-blowing stargazing, plan your trip during a new moon to be fully blown away by the night lights. Conversely, if you wish for better sleep when a bright moon rises at 11 p.m., your fly can help with that. It's incredible how bright a full moon can be and how it can affect your sleep.

If you want to sleep when the wind whips up and pelts your tent with pine needles or the thunderhead rolls through with quick-moving sprinkles, add your rainfly.

It only takes once waking up to rain spitting in your face through the netting to realize that fumbling around via headlamp at 3 a.m. in a race to keep your gear dry is far from the macho of going without a rainfly.

Ditch Some Stakes

Modern tents come with all the stakes you'll need if you peg each corner and each optional guy line if high winds are expected. Sometimes an extra stake or two is included, for which I am grateful. I lose them regularly. But never once have I hiked with them all. Take your tent out for a spin and take the challenge to see how many stakes you can do *without*. They are a weighty part of the shelter system. Leave some stakes behind, knowing you can innovate with a stick or a stone for non-critical corners. Depending on design, an easy way to ditch a few stakes is by using your rainfly to pin your tent body down with pressure. With both tent body and fly staked completely, start removing body stakes in the corners held taut by poles. Between taut corner poles, your gear inside, and the downward pressure of the staked fly, the tent body isn't going anywhere, even in a windstorm.

I've rarely felt the need to use upper guy lines to brace against wind. But when I've needed them, I don't find it practical to stake them into the ground. The steep downward angle of the cordage isn't ideal. Where possible, it works better to pin it to a high boulder or sturdy tree. High winds typically come from one direction. Don't be afraid to untie excess cordage from the leeward side of your tent to double the distance on the windward. This helps to hitch horizontally on far away anchors. Hang a caution hanky to the new tripwire.

Stakes Before Poles

If your tent body needs stakes regardless, or if you're savvy enough to pull them out later to use elsewhere on the fly, make your life easier by staking the tent before clipping in your poles. Tents can be assembled either way successfully—poles first or stakes first. But that satisfying taut nylon feeling comes when stakes are set first. By the time I'm done with the fly, I want my home to be trampoline-tight. When rain or morning dew hits the fabric, it loosens. This droops your fly and causes it to adhere to the tent body. And a taut tent is also far quieter when the wind kicks up.

Conversely, if you have had the sad experience of packing up a wet tent in the morning and later setting up damp fabric, don't stake the fabric too tight. The nylon fly will shrink and stiffen as it dries.

Find Your Hip Hole

Before you commit to a tent spot, kick a few pinecones and circle it like a dog getting ready to rest. Squat like a golfer on a green to understand the grade direction. This helps you see where your head and feet should go or how water might move through. More than once, I've foolishly set up my tent, and eagerly jumped in, only to feel an unseen lump bulging right into my kidney. To move the tent at that point requires removing stakes and starting again.

To prevent this, lay down directly on the grass — or better yet, on your ground cloth — and shift around, feeling for the right hip hole. A hip hole is a slight depression where your butt will reside if you're on your back, and your hip will sit when side-sleeping. Sure, you have a proper pad that will remove the little bumps. But you're trying to find favorable contours. If there's a high spot, you want it on the small of your back or behind your head.

How-to books will teach you to avoid sleeping in a low spot, as rain may gather there. That may be the case if it rains all night, but most topsoil in the backcountry eagerly absorbs rain unless your site is by assignment or commonly used. The more the area is used, the greater chance that pooling might be a problem, as compacted soil helps rainfall travel. The small curve in the earth you're looking for is not an obvious low spot in the meadow where water collects. Remember, even in the worst-case scenario, the tent floor is waterproof, as is the ground cloth. More often than not, your primary concern should be adjusting for slope sleeping rather than preventing puddles.

I prefer a slight grade to perfectly flat ground. Keep your head uphill, and don't be afraid of a slope that drops off dramatically where your feet will fall. This imitates having your feet dangling off the edge of the bed at home. (Perhaps that's just a tall-person problem.)

All this prep may sound like excessive analysis and borderline neurotic, but on average, you're committing to eight to ten hours lying on that piece of earth. After a physical day of punching over a pass or casting a line until dusk overtakes vision, I've been known to crash hard and sleep eleven or twelve hours. You're on vacation. Allow yourself the same.

Take a few extra minutes to maximize comfort. When your pad is installed and your bag laid out, the goal is for you to stretch out your bones on it for a moment of exhaling and exclaim, "Yeah, that's nice. I may just lay here for a bit."

Power nap.

Reduce Upside-Down Rain

One of the few cons of sleeping snug under the rainfly is the risk of waking up on a still morning to condensation. Solution one: stop breathing so much.

Maybe let's look at other solutions.

Start by using stakes the way they were designed by not pinning the corners to the forest floor. Tent body stakes are intended to be pushed flush with the earth, but rainfly stakes are meant to stick up an inch or two to create an updraft under the edge. Test ventilation by reaching your arm under to touch your tent. While you're in there, pull out the corners of your ground cloth. Next, grab a good-sized rock, place it next to your stake or under the corner of the fabric, pinning it down. I just saved you a trip—literally. The brain recognizes rocks as something to avoid tripping over more than a skinny piece of aluminum and cord, especially when stumbling around your tent after dark. I'm talking to you, 3 a.m. potty break.

Another fix: use the double zipper built with tent doorways. I've seen campers who never notice that the door to their vestibule may have a second zipper hidden at the top, whose sole purpose is venting. Create a vent by pulling both zippers partway down, and then running the lower zipper to the ground to close up shop. The upper gap catches the breeze and cuts the moisture.

Third solution: if it's a mild night, sleep with the door open until you're cool. Tent flies are built with a tie to keep the door fabric from flapping free. Condensation collects at the coldest time of night—right before daybreak. Reduce it by creating your own giant vent. When it gets too cold or starts sprinkling, rather than exiting your cozy bag to stake a fly together, just roll over and zip it closed. Summer nights start a bit warmer than preferred. Sliding in a warm down bag exaggerates the temperature. There's a satisfaction to falling asleep with a generous open-door breeze and an arm out, then being awoken with a cold shoulder. I love zipping up the fly and disappearing deeper into my bag about midnight.

Each campsite location has a different mix of tree cover, night breezes, and cold air pockets, all of which affect the likelihood of the interior drip. When you have choices for campsites, which will be discussed later, real estate rules matter. Location, location, location.

Sometimes no matter what you do or where you settle, condensation is unavoidable. Consider it a part of great weather. When I wake up to condensation, it's a blessing and a curse. Mild weather awaits that morning but flopping the fly upside down on a boulder or branch to dry before packing is a chore. I'd much rather awake to calm condensation than the pitter-patter of a morning shower.

Use Your Vestibule

Protected vestibules created by the angled rainfly are underused, which makes engineers who designed them get sad. Treat each night as though it's going to rain for a few hours. Placing your pack under a tree is good, but using a vestibule is better. By bedtime, my vestibule hosts what remains of my pack, a pair of stinky shoes airing out with the insoles removed, and my water bladder.

While I'm on that topic, never bring water, especially hydration hoses, into your tent. The risks of an inadvertent leak are too high, and your sleeping bag quickly becomes a sponge. You make that mistake only once. Treat water like a flame around tents. The vestibule is the perfect spot for water as it's an arms-length solution for taking meds from the comfort of your bag or awaking parched under the stars.

Another trick is to set up your boots unlaced with insoles removed. This not only gives them a chance to air out overnight—hopefully with a breeze making it under the fly and carrying the smell away—but gives you night slippers. Your feet slide more easily into boots without insoles. Coordination needs every bit of help when you need to shuffle around in the dark outside your tent for a potty break. Tough guys prefer walking on bare feet on the forest floors. Tough guys also track sticky pine pitch and grit back into their bag.

Morning Chores

Regardless of exterior dew or interior condensation, one of the first chores of the morning is to get that constrictive fly off. Morning sunshine is typical in the summer as clouds build during the heat of the day. This works out perfectly for drying gear before the next leg of the course. While rubbing your eyes to wake up, get the fly into full sun, whether laid like a blanket on a slab of stone or dangling from a branch. Give it a shake and flip it like a pancake. Don't spread it in meadow grass, as that can be deceivingly wet.

The fly-off-first habit also allows easier access to organizing your messy tent floor without working through a constrictive vestibule door. By the time you've assembled most of your pack and finished your oatmeal, the rainfly should be thoroughly cooked to a crisp. If it's not, don't sweat it. A few wet spots won't hurt you and will dry once set back up later that day. Don't get paralyzed waiting for dry perfection. It's more important to get moving before cumulus clouds assemble. Better to carry some wetness and set up before the afternoon auto sprinklers kick on.

Before packing the body of the tent away, remove the stakes but keep the poles attached. Pick the tent up by its spine with the doors wide open and heft it over your head. Do a little dance and shake out the corners allowing the debris to escape. Zip up all the doors on the body and fly before punching it into its sack. Tents erect much easier — and tighter — without floppy doors.

Sleep System

A bag and a pad — these two have been the industry standard for decades. Lately, there are interesting new hybrids like pads that insert into your bag to avoid slippage. Some "bags" are more like quilts and require attachment to a pad. The theory is to avoid wasting good goose down otherwise crushed underneath your body. Whatever your combination, consider your climate first.

The Catch-22s of sleeping bags are fascinating. Each type of fill has its own superpower and kryptonite. When I moved to the mossy Pacific Northwest, I had recently converted my go-to bags to high-end down designed for the arid climate of Rocky Mountain ranges. I quickly learned that humidity and down are sworn enemies. Down struggles in high humidity as it absorbs moisture out of the air, loses loft, and loses efficacy.

Conversely, polyester-filled bags can retain warmth even if the sky is soggy or if the bag itself gets soaked. They are quicker to dry than down and priced lower but can be twice the weight and half as compressible. A quality down bag will be lighter, more compressible, and more expensive, but compromised if exposed to rain. Depending on where you wander, start with the right fill. Compare humidity and the likelihood of rain. Then compare costs, weight, and size. Some bags are being made with both types of stuffing to offer a hybrid solution.

Roll with It

How you sleep in your bag is up to you, whether on your back, side, or face. But after trying several ways, I recommend rolling with it—meaning, treat your bag as a giant fluffy onesie. When you move, bend your knees and roll the whole bag with you. (This advice only applies to bags unattached to their pad.)

Habitually, we do the opposite and treat bags like our bed at home, where you roll *within* the covers. But spinning your body inside of a slender mummy bag is a recipe for a midnight wedgie. Whatever you wear to sleep will quickly twist uncomfortably and ride up into cracks and pits. It also wrenches the crucial fluff out of the warming baffles and risks claustrophobic feelings with the zipper inaccessible against your back. Rolling the bag with your body keeps your zipper within reach and the hood wrapped around the backend of your head like it was designed. The only time you'll enjoy your hood in your face is if the sun shows up too early. Then it's a lifesaver.

Your pillow, whether inflatable or a wad of clothing jammed into a stuff sack, can tuck nicely into your hood. The hood keeps it in place. How convenient! But that's only convenient if you're warm enough to sleep with your head outside the bag's hood or when you're a back sleeper.

Instead, put the pillow on your pad—*outside* the bag—and use the hood as if it were part of a jacket. If you're too hot too often when using the hood, that's a clue you're needlessly hefting too much bag.

Aaron and I have wandered for hundreds of miles together, much to the chagrin of our loving wives. In our early years of clumsy gear choices, he would repeatedly complain about how hot he slept. It would keep him up at night sapping his strength the next day. He'd strip down nearly naked to make it through a night in his massive down cocoon and blame it on himself. Leaving the zipper halfway down or sticking a leg out was his only relief. On day three, I finally asked him what the bag's temperature rating was. He looked at the tag and admitted, "Negative thirty." I'm sure my jaw opened. He realized the overkill. A bag built for the Arctic was innocently purchased—and hefted—for summer trips in the Rockies. That was the bag's last adventure.

Fully Dressed for Success

Proponents of ultralight theory recommend carrying as light of a bag as you can stand. Lighter bags equate to higher temperature tolerances between 30 and 40 degrees. Advocates recommend if you're still chilly, wear the layers you're already carrying to bed; thus, no weight gets wasted. Makes sense.

Two different summers, I tested this theory and carried a tiny, 19-ounce, 40-degree bag throughout cooler high elevations. One summer, I took one brand, then traded it, hoping another brand would work better. These bags packed down impossibly small. I also had a delightful down jacket I donned. The plan was to use them together. The results were mixed. Nights worked out well enough wearing a long-sleeve stretchy base layer under my down jacket inside the 850-fill down bag using the bag's hood as well. But occasionally, when a cold front would move through, or I was camped in a valley bottom where cold air settled, I would still wake up shivering. (Granted, I sleep chilly outside and at home.) It also bothered me to wear my good down jacket, with its fitted form, all night. The slender body would twist out of place. The inside collar got greasy against my neck skin. I felt like I wasn't doing it any favors with excessive wear.

The third summer, I abandoned hopes of making a 40-degree bag my summer go-to. A 30-degree bag was a few ounces more but paired with a long-sleeve top and a pair of sexy stretchy tights, it hit the spot—one of several examples of trying ultralight theory until sensibility steps in, then backing off a bit. That's being pragmatic.

As you shop for a bag, be aware of what's inside. All polyester fill isn't created equal. Nor is all down. There's goose down ranging from the affordable and adequate 600- or 650-fill range to more elite and expensive 800- or 850-fills. Some are made with duck down or a blend. Lower grades have feathers mixed in. I've used all types, and they're all respectable. But gram counters will want to pony up for the higher-end—and much lighter—goose downs. The higher the grade of down, the smaller it will compress. You get what you pay for here. Quality bags will last years if stored properly.

Polyesters and other synthetics are becoming more advanced each year with increased waterproofing, weight savings, and improved loft—the right choice when you're hiking among the ferns of the Pacific Northwest or other humid forests of hardwoods.

The Sleeping Pad Conundrum

The lightest sleeping pads are made of thin or egg-crate closed-cell foam. They nudge the postal scale at 10-12 ounces. They are indestructible, waterproof, and can be comfortably placed on rocky ledges for an instant butt pad. Versatile, yes. Comfortable and compact, not so much.

One weeklong adventure with my teenagers, I got to our first campsite and cracked open my pack to start nesting. Much to my horror, I realized my favorite two-inch-thick inflatable pad was snug in the trunk at the trailhead. Amateur mistake: disassembling and reassembling your pack at the trailhead when the rest of the group is hot to trot. Leave it alone or risk leaving something behind. Trailheads are terribly exciting but a high-risk leave-something-in-the-car trap. Sunglasses top the list.

Speaking of leaving something in the car: leave the keys. There's no need nor added safety gained by hiking a set of keys around all week. They add weight and puncture risk. Instead, walk a few steps around your vehicle and look for a prominent stone or shrub. Creatively hide your keys under an unforgettable rock or log. Tell your hiking buddy. God forbid they have to return to the car without you, or for your medical help, they'll have the keys ready.

Reflecting on what I had left at the car forced me to accept my consequence—I had to sleep on the ground all week and just survive. I did a bit better, gathering a few closed-cell butt pad pieces the group had packed for sitting. Aligned together under my bag with all my spare clothing, I had barely enough to cover my bony skeleton hinge points—hips and shoulders. Ibuprofen did the rest, and I got through it. I nearly threw my forgotten pad across the parking lot upon return. It wasn't my first time trying to use thin foam for bedding, but I hope it was my last.

The sleeping pad conundrum isn't just about comfort; it's about the next day. Weeklong treks are physically challenging. One night of inadequate sleep isn't the end of the world for hardy hikers, but when you need your body on the second day to hammer over a high pass, sleep becomes more than a gram contest. Trip success depends on it!

In my experience, the younger the body, the more likely the person will be able to brush off the padding consequences of a closed-cell pad. The older the body, the more it becomes an issue.

For a better night's rest, it's worth adding a few ounces. High-end inflatable pads run 12-15 ounces. Several more affordable options are in the 16- to 20-ounce range. For a mere two- to four-ounce upgrade, you can go from egg-crate foam to two-inches of warm, bouncy bliss. I've survived on one and thrived on the other.

And lest we forget the space savings. Another glaring trade-off of the closed-cell option is the boxy bulk. Rolled up, they become a 20-inch-long cubic rectangle or cylinder, limited to an exterior attachment on your pack. Strike two. Compare that to the nine-inch length of a rolled-up inflatable that easily disappears inside.

The bulk of rolled or folded closed-cell foam pads thwart the efforts and grace of an otherwise slender pack. Bushwhack-savvy packs are core-sized—no lower than your hips, no taller than your ears, and no broader than your ribcage. When looking head-on, a proper setup nearly disappears behind the hiker's upper body. Small packs aren't for style, but for comfort in mobility, promoting safety with better balance, natural arm swing, and branch-snag reduction. Also eliminated: inadvertently knocking the Nalgene bottle out of your buddy's hands while turning your girthy gear around. As much as I envy the weight savings, I can't look past the obtrusive bulk attached atop (or below) an otherwise back-sized pack.

The Perfect Pack

Brian Regan is a fantastic stand-up comedian. In one of his bits, he surmised a refrigerator salesman's needless job by imitating his sales pitch. Pointing at the first fridge, he explains, "This one keeps your food cold for $600. *[He walks to the next one.]* You've got this refrigerator right here. This one keeps your food cold for $800. *[Walks to the next one.]* Check this out. $1,400. Keeps your food cold."

When you shop for packs, view it the same. This one carries your stuff for $200. This one carries your stuff for $300, and so forth. The advantages of higher-end packs are typically needless compartments and features that promise convenience, but more regularly add weight and complication, similar to the "meats drawer" the salesman is selling in Regan's bit. (If you haven't watched it already, I recommend it.)

Packs are designed for one purpose: to carry your stuff comfortably. View it as simple as that, and you'll save money and complexity. Luckily, it's difficult to buy a bad one these days. They are incredibly comfortable, and each brand has one in each carrying capacity. They're nothing like the rickety external-frame packs of the 80s. You can hardly buy an external frame any longer. Modern rigid plastic frames are hidden internally and spread the load against your back. Unlike a few years ago, when typical models offered lower compartments recommended for sleeping bags, most designs these days are essentially a singular, vertical, compressible cylinder. It's like carrying a giant compression sack on your back. Models are becoming narrower and more streamlined, with cleaner lines and fewer exterior pockets. The carrier is expected to do more of their own organization internally and be less dependent on individual compartments. Not to worry; it's nothing a few mesh ditty bags or resealable baggies can't solve.

Buy your pack last, after you're set on your shelter and sleep system. As you're evaluating, upgrading, or lightening your gear, don't start with the pack—hence why I'm addressing it at the end. Use what you have. Beg, borrow, or steal from a friend until you have the other pieces of your trifecta; only nomads are using their pack every week. And unlike borrowing a sleeping bag, which can feel a little personal, borrowing a pack until you know your needs is a great way to test drive. Shrink your tent. Shrink your bag and pad. Once those are done, you'll reveal your actual capacity needs.

Look for packs with stretchy external pockets. They're useful for the list of exterior-friendly items above. Don't get stressed if a model doesn't include a traditional lid or other pouches. Minimal packs are lidless. An essentials sack stuffed under a rolled pack top serves the same purpose and can more easily join you in the corner of the tent when you're needing some lip balm or earplugs. Osprey, REI, and a few other brands make reasonably light and affordable packs, but brands like Granite Gear and Gossamer Gear are designing lightweight packs that check all the boxes of durability, simplicity, and price.

As for pack covers, you'll stop carrying one as you notice your pack is built to be water-resistant itself, and nearly everything in your set-up is made of quick-dry materials— or should be. What remains should be shelled in its own water-resistant stuff sack or sealed in a resealable baggie. If it rains intensely, it's time to duck under a tree or don a grocery store disposable poncho that can flop over your pack and be tucked into straps to cut down the flapping. These cheap covers are great for a few uses. On each week, you can count on one of three outcomes: it never gets opened, it's used once during a hellacious hailstorm, or it gets used a few times and peppered with holes by week's end. Worst case, you're out 99 cents but have no stress compared to owning a damaged custom pack cover. And these disposable ponchos are great over lightweight rain jackets. It seems redundantly odd until you try it.

How Big Is Big?

Generally speaking, 75- to 90-liter packs are for heavy-duty needs in big game hunting or climbing expeditions. 55- to 75-liter packs are for average weeklong journeys. Strive to get near the bottom of this range, or even better, into the sweet 45- to 55-liter class. These are pleasant to pack and more possible when you're divvying gear among a group.

A fair way to split gear between two is to have one carry the tent's hardware (stakes and poles) while the other lugs the fabric (body, fly, ground cloth). Additional shared gear can be divided by one carrying the stove system and the other, the water filter. The weight distribution is never entirely fair, but the method takes care of some noticeable bulky shared gear. Sharing is a practical way to minimize pack capacity needs.

One may argue that it's easier to buy a larger pack just in case you need it. I recommend the opposite. Buy the smallest capacity you can reasonably get away with on a weeklong trip. The worst-case scenario is you have items clipped to the exterior for the first day or two, like a tent or jacket, until your food bag is whittled down a bit, allowing other things to fit later. This also "forces" you to push yourself and your gear list toward a smaller and simpler set-up. Larger packs give the false invitation that you could—and therefore should—take more since there's room remaining.

Once you've decided what gear should be divvied among friends, segregate the durable articles that can be safely strapped to the pack exterior. The shortlist of equipment that could ride best on the outside includes camp/creek shoes, tent poles, fishing rod, water, repellent, raingear, hat, handkerchief, pad (if foam), and a tent. Not all of these need to be outside each time but treat them as economy passengers if the plane is sold out. If there's an unexpected extra seat in the front of the interior cabin, select one for an upgrade to first class.

The litmus test: "If I set my stuff down in the sticks or bushwhack or lean against a tree, will I be puncturing anything that would need a patch?"

The hard, durable stuff goes best on the exterior, so the soft, compressible elements can get smashed into the interior.

Stretch the Seams

When smashing your soft stuff into the fancy long tube they call a pack, build the bottom first. Ensure any horizontal compression straps are loose to start. Begin with your bag, pad, and/or tent set vertically like foundational columns. Upright stuff sacks conform to the curves of the pack and create gaps to fill between the cylinders. Build this first bulky foundation layer until the walls are nearly bursting at the seams. Don't do damage, but don't "move up" to the next layer until you plug that void between your bag and your pad with underwear or socks you won't need today, or your clean sleeping shirt. It's astonishing how many rolled-up pieces of clothing can get stuffed into cracks if you try. Once you've utilized every void around your foundational items, move up to the next layer until it's stretched tight. My second layer is primarily clothing and small gear. The goal isn't to strain your seams; it's to utilize every single cubic inch in a game of fabric Tetris. Whistling your own Russian folk music as you go is up to you.

It's less critical to pack the top half as flawlessly as you sometimes need to root around in there during the day like a raccoon for a snack. Essentials, toiletries, and food go at the top of the pack.

Cameron's below-the-neck roll-top pack is slender and promotes upright posture.

With practice, you'll know how things best fit in what order and can fill it blindfolded. Something is satisfying about having a smooth-sided, slender, stuffed pack. It looks inflated like a catalog product image photo—like it was meant to be. It calls out to you, "I'm ready. Let's go somewhere!"

CHAPTER 5
ROUTE PLANNING

There's no shortage of where-to-go recommendations. Outdoor books, magazine articles, forum posts, and social media photos abound, screaming their top destination ideas and suggestions. It's a great big world out there with limitless options if you have the resources to travel abroad. But even staying closer to home requires responsible planning of hours required to get to the trailhead, hours on the trail, and days it will take to make the trip click. This book won't outline routes, but I can't resist putting in a plug for the beautiful places I've been blessed to behold.

This counsel comes from expeditions in the national forests, wilderness areas, and public lands of the Rocky Mountains of Utah, Wyoming, Montana, and Colorado and a decade living near the lush Cascade Mountains of Oregon. With their near-opposite climates and weather patterns, these two distinctive ecosystems give proven credibility to the tested pragmatic approach.

I've also backpacked the sandstone slot canyons of the Southwest. These desert lands have their appeal with thousands, but for me, the alpine call of gushing spring water flowing into waving wildflowers below glacier-carved cirques draws me back to the mountains each summer— although I realize desert locales can promise springs, blooms, and towering canyons as well!

Wildflowers flourish above the timberline near Elbow Peak (11,988 ft).

I've Got Plans That Week

Route design can be as entertaining as experiencing the actual expedition in-person—almost. Connecting lines between trailheads and the backcountry takes weeks (or months) and cures winter blues in cold climates. A deliberate design also ensures you carve out the best weeks for which adventures in your calendar. Live by the mantra "If it's not calendared, it doesn't exist." You can have all the best routes in the best locales in the world in mind, but until you protect them with a block of days in your calendar, they will never be realized. Summer trips are easily forecasted in the winter or spring, but to combine with another's work schedule, or bring a group together, sometimes pinning the right dates nearly a year ahead is required. If not, something else will inevitably take its place.

Know Before You Go

By the time you set boots on a trail, research it in so many ways you feel like you've already walked it. Planning is a proactive way to experience the terrain vicariously before you arrive. It also decreases easy oversights, like terrain barriers or other on-ground surprises. Previewing reveals discernable campsites and opens off-trail opportunities. Know more than the distance. Paper maps are valuable but limit knowing serviceable groundcover. Satellite imagery from online sources reveals vegetation, tricky talus fields, inviting meadows, bogs to dodge, and wildfire scars not shown on paper. This technology is free, viewable in 3D, and offers an incredible advantage only available in the last decade. Use it.

I've had entire routes redrawn because of what satellite imagery displayed. I was zoomed in on a high lake nestled in its own remote granite cirque and noticed both the east and west shorelines were cliffed out. The shoreline was impassable without risking an icy—or deadly—plunge. Topo maps are dependable and rarely let me down, but I'm glad I looked closer. This research saved me from being boxed into a vast canyon and either having to retrace my steps into the neighboring valley or traverse vertically over a narrow ridgeline.

Other times, I've been successful in predicting where fresh spring water will be accessible right when I need it by looking at slope and vegetation patterns. Images can show what corner of the valley has advantageous tree cover for camping or strategic shorelines for fishing. Satellite imagery can also expose the trail's actual path as these are rerouted but rarely redrawn on paper maps. Numerous dotted-black-line trails on the USGS maps were accurate only when drawn 40 or 60 years ago. Consult multiple online resources to confirm trail accuracy. The USGS originals are great for particular uses, but private map makers have modern updates.

Going Rogue

Only a handful of times have I found myself backpacking blind, meaning I hadn't poured over every switchback and junction. This method is invigorating in its own way but has risks.

One three-day 32-mile loop, I was forced to operate off photos of maps stored on my phone. It was a course I hadn't planned as my perfectly plotted weeklong loop ended early after equipment failures and a few disheartening mistakes. The mountain forced me to an early exit. I licked my wounds and regrouped at a different trailhead, ready to punch back into the wild toward a different set of lakes. I didn't know where I would be camping the first night. I took on the role of renegade and tried to be uncharacteristically spontaneous.

Five miles in, I stepped off the trail to allow a horseman by. The sun was getting low. He asked where I was camping that night and, for the first time in my life, I couldn't answer him with exactness. Instead, I smugly said, "Not sure yet. I'm gonna see how far I get before dark."

He smiled approvingly, "That's the best way to do it."

I was proud of myself for breaking my usual mold of exactness and precision.

Nightfall neared, and I found myself quickening my pace along a large lake to find any morsel of terrain not peppered with boulders that could fit a tiny tent. A dusty patch was discovered. The tent was placed by headlamp. Awoken by footsteps the next morning, I exited my olive tent to stretch and noticed my spot was eight feet from the main trail, not ideal.

Another unexpected consequence of my haphazard plan: I didn't notice that day two—technically day five considering the previous trip—would require a 16-mile hoof to arrive at the second lake. I woke up the last day with a strained Achilles heel caused by sheer overuse. It stung to the touch. The last several miles had me gingerly limping down the trail wearing a black foam sandal on my right foot. This solution was the only relief I could find as my boot's stiff uppers were too painful against the tendon.

The excellent fishing experienced that route was well worth the unknowns and the injury. Your spontaneous trips will hopefully end happier. They are exciting, but the pragmatic in me is reminded to do real research each time. Fortunately, I enjoy map reading.

Get Contour Crazy

That last sentence was a lie. I'm *obsessed* with the art of maps. As a teenager, I was first introduced to topographic maps and was instantly enamored. I viewed contour lines in three dimensions. It felt like I was unlocking a code. As a teenager, I'd take a bus downtown to the only place that stored every topo map statewide. It wasn't a public library or an outdoor retailer. It was a federal building where the USGS was housed. There was a dark, quiet backroom straight out of a mystery movie. It was lined wall-to-wall with wide, shallow drawers, each with ten copies of the 7.5-minute quadrangle maps developed in the 1970s. Sorted alphabetically, I navigated as many printouts as I'd like, pulling each out onto a well-lit table and imagining what standing on those slopes would be like—or *will* be. I must have been the only teenager who frequented the repository.

With the onset of online mapping, topographic maps have become more useful and user-friendly. Seamless panning relieves the planner from folding and aligning awkward map borders. Relief shading adds depth. Satellite imagery layers can be mixed in for terrain context. Trails can be traced and adjusted digitally with distance measurements and automatic elevation profiles. It's a candy store for hobby cartographers.

No matter the format, paper or online, route design follows similar rules regardless if you're planning in New Zealand or New Mexico. Similar questions surface about how many miles the group can attempt each day or what miles-per-hour will be covered. You may have a goal like a peak or a lake. Then you build around it.

Backpacking has countless appeals. There are results-oriented goals like access to remote climbing walls, summiting the highest peaks, or catching trout in a backcountry setting. There are also personal goals like photography, serenity, outdoorsmanship, or just being "out there" with friends and family. With your goal in mind, you'll start carving out the days it will demand.

Budgeting Miles

Do yourself a favor. Be cautious and conservative when budgeting miles per day. The number one mistake seen in doomed agendas is too many miles planned than the person or group can tackle. When time off puts pressure on the mileage covered per day, you're asking for trouble. Increase your days off or drop your distance. If not, rather than enjoying the trail, you'll be tapping your watch, hurrying at the trailhead, and racing the sun to the horizon. Every delay, every rest, every slow RV on the highway in front of you adds anxiety.

Instead, operate with this mantra in mind: "Everything is going to take longer than I think. And that's okay."

Someone in the group won't be ready. Others may need to adjust their gear along the trail. Something will be forgotten and in need of purchase on the way. It's so much more enjoyable to arrive on the first night's campsite and have two or three extra hours to kill than the converse because you didn't over budget.

Groups travel slower than solo trekkers. Youth or those new to backpacking will have a shorter stride than experienced adults. Budget a conservative 1.5 miles per hour for novice companies heading uphill on day one. On a steady downgrade along a well-maintained trail at the other end of the spectrum, one or two practiced hikers can comfortably clock three or four miles per hour, assuming ideal conditions and hurried breaks. Considering rocky terrain and complications of elevation, those bursts of speed are rare. Realistically, two miles per hour is a steady pace midweek, factoring in enjoyable breaks, and the natural leap-frogging groups experience.

First Day and Last Day

Be patient with day one. The first day will be the hardest. It will be the one day with the most massive pack as no food has been eaten and water containers are maxed. It will feel the slowest as legs, lungs, and gear are not quite in sync. It will hike the slowest as "heading to the hills" is literally guaranteeing walking a lot of uphill on day one.

Backpacking typically assumes entering a mountain range—the rare exception is a day-one downhill drop into a remote gorge. Groups need a day to discover the pace and hiking order of who likes to lead and who's on wrapper pick-up duty in the rear. Lastly, day one generally includes picking up the group and driving hours to the trailhead. Logistics are rarely smooth or punctual. Plan on getting to the trailhead later than you'd like. Be pleasantly surprised otherwise.

Conversely, the last days, especially on weeklong journeys, feel completely different. Packs are several pounds lighter without a week's rations. They are more refined and better packed with daily practice. Stops are fewer as legs, lungs, and straps are operating in sync and altitude acclimated. The best part: you're walking downhill. Sorry, canyoneers. You had your easy day.

Be conservative with your early day mileage expectations and liberal with the latter. Need to punch out double the miles on the last day? Plan on it. The horse will smell the barn, in this case, a hot shower, and you'll rarely stop to sit.

After exploring hundreds of miles solo, and several group expeditions with youth and family, I've arrived at the sweet spot of expecting six to eight uphill miles from a group on day one, then increasing distances as needed during the week. The larger the group, the shorter the mileage on day one. When solo, I can comfortably punch double those lengths if required, but I typically don't get a lot from my legs after the 14-mile mark. I've done a few days in the high teens to 20, but it ends up uncomfortable. You'll need to discover your own range. Much of this varies by terrain and physical prep.

Consider other activities than miles per day. One lake might be perfect for an afternoon swim. Another area may need extra time for switchbacks or an off-trail scramble. If you're marching all day every day without purpose; you're going to burn out of the sport, unless your goal is a cross-continental thru-hike. The hike-all-day adventure is an entirely different style of backpacking. It's more athletic, can regularly cover 20-30 miles per day depending on terrain, requires more precise gear considerations, and a whole other guidebook.

Lollipops are Sweet: Types of Backcountry Routes

After decades of drawing lines to the next destination, I've noticed all backcountry routes fall into one of three types: the classic out-and-back, the more logistic-laden thru-hike, and the sweet-spot lollipop loop. Each has strengths and drawbacks to deliberate.

Out-and-backs are how the majority experience their backpacking beginnings. Park here. Hike to the camp. Hike back. These can be kid-friendly, simple five-mile roundtrip romps. They can also be 55-mile expeditions over ear-popping passes, soggy glaciers, and include off-trail bushwhacking. No matter the distance or terrain, there's a point midweek where the map turns you around, and you experience everything a second time, but in reverse.

The vital point is obvious—it's the easiest to plan and execute. The drawback is that 50% of it can feel old hat. It's not instantly boring to retrace your steps, and hindsight hiking can be more relaxing, as you know what to expect, where water is best sourced, or where the sweet spot is to crash for the night. But it's remarkable how a little variety can enhance the journey and switch up the scenery. For a three-night route where you have a campsite halfway there, at the destination, then halfway back again, make an effort to camp that third night somewhere new. Try the other side of the lake or a mile further down the trail.

Thru-hiking entails hiking from point A to point B. It can be a cross-section course or an arch to a neighboring trailhead. This is a marvelous way to travel, as each step is unique and never repeated as you move through the terrain. You don't have the restrictive feeling in the back of your mind that you have to turn around at a certain point. Instead, you can keep punching into new drainages daily. Thru-hiking is easily accomplished with a second car and shuttling plans, although, it's a little heavy on logistics and prep time.

It's best to have both vehicles fit all people and gear, but thru-hiking can be accomplished with less seating depending on distance and patience. For example, a less-than-ideal arrangement may involve part of the group bouncing down a dusty access road in the bed of a truck. Bed surfing may be your only choice if the last few miles are rough and the other vehicle is best parked where pavement ends and potholes begin. You'll start your week dustier than you'd prefer, but you are backpacking after all.

Another option: have someone who owes you a big favor drop you off or pick you up days later at an arranged time. Paid shuttle services are also sometimes offered between trailheads, similar to local guiding services. They can move your car while you're on the trail or drive you from your exit to your entry.

Don't make this shuttling mistake, however. After designing an exciting 45-mile arching thru-hike for a family group, I noticed that the last couple of miles of one of the two trailheads were rutted dirt road and accessible only by high-clearance vehicles. It was decided to take the sedan to the paved trailhead parking lot, then all could jump in the SUV over to the rugged entry point. However, that plan only worked for the *beginning* of the trip. The thru-hike was a huge success, but when driving back to the starting point to retrieve the SUV, we remembered the low-clearance sedan wouldn't make it up the rugged road. After finishing a weeklong trek, my legs were spent—but I wasn't done. My only choice was to take the car as far as its muffler would allow, then hike the last couple miles of rough dirt road with the SUV keys in one hand and a half-liter of water in the other. It all worked out in the end, but real-world experience—and basic logic—would've helped prevent that hiccup. Moral of the story? Both cars need to be able to access both trailheads.

Although not dependable, thru-hikes can also be completed by hitchhiking, which is more courteous and safer to do at the outset. You'll find you'll be quicker to be trusted with a ride when your hair is combed on day one than the grizzly, tattered, and smelly person you become while thumbing at your exit.

Lollipop routes are the sweet spot between out-and-backs and thru-hikes. I call them lollipop loops, as that's what the itinerary creates when drawn on a map. They've become my preferred methods of route planning. Using one trailhead for logistical ease, find a trail that splits soon afterward—the sooner, the better to avoid retracing steps. Then proceed off the fork into a wandering path over ridges and valleys. These round routes have all the ease of one vehicle, one trailhead, and one driver but provide unique travel each day. Ideal lollipops can be designed with shortcuts or just-in-case routes.

Want to spend more time at an exceptionally productive fishing spot? Or, heaven forbid, do you have an equipment failure and need to exit early?

Good routes have alternates lines drawn to lengthen or shorten the loop, adding day hikes to extend one way or cut-offs to close up shop. This option gives an advantage over thru-hikes, which have more pressure on completing the full course. Of course, any trip can be cut short for emergencies, but thru-hikes have transportation arrangements that are difficult to change unexpectedly midway.

The only small drawback: lollipop loops are more physically challenging. They require a commitment of at least two or three nights and typically involve popping over a pass between drainages to close the circuit. Enjoy this challenge as it gives variety and scenery changes.

Off-Trail is Off-The-Hook

A common complaint with travel is crowds. We all want to travel, whether to national parks, theme parks, or the campground, without dealing with the multitudes who had the exact same idea on the same day. Backpacking is a proven way to break away, but you still have to be a bit creative.

I once hiked past a high-use lake a good five miles from a crowded trailhead. It was the week before school started, a popular window for a last-week-of-the-summer trek. As I circumnavigated the busy shoreline on the way to a less-used lake beyond, I decided to make a headcount. I counted 42 folks before I stopped—and those are the ones I could see in passing. There were clearly more in tents and out of view. If I was not careful or did less planning, I would've driven a few hours on my day off to backpack five miles uphill only to spend the evening on a lake in a wilderness area with 42 other people.

That is unacceptable.

The second lake, less than two extra miles uphill, had eight others camped sparsely along its slopes. I sat on a rock overlooking the lake during the sunset, watching tiny trout rise and the orange alpenglow illuminate the granite wall above me. The few who were there were kept to themselves.

It was as though I had the place all to myself. The next day, it got even better. As I marched off-trail into different drainages beyond those first two lakes, I didn't see another soul for two days.

Getting off-trail is one of the quickest ways to have the wild to yourself. When my boys were old enough to tote their own school backpack, they immediately started off-trail backpacking. One little lake I targeted was stocked with tiger trout. It required a mere half-mile of trail plus one mile off-trail through a broken forest and mild meadows. Even though this spot was only one-and-a-half miles from a major highway and packed trailhead parking lot, we never once fought for a campsite nor shared the lake with another group. It was our own private paradise, and we returned to it for a few summers.

Off-trail exploration requires practice, confidence, and, most importantly, the right groundcover. No one likes to bushwhack like you're swimming in brush for miles nor pick through loose talus for too long. But the broken forests and open high country above the tree line of the Rocky Mountains are ideal for escaping the trodden paths. Once at altitude, your options become infinite. Rather than being confined to official trails, you can open your stride across tundra-topped plateaus and pop over welcoming saddles between peaks.

When off-trail, you can choose to feel pleasantly relieved or disappointed when you find yourself on an unmapped use trail or game trail heading the same way. There are hundreds of these, as you are not the first hiker or elk to think up this route. One part of you may have hoped it to be more primitive. The other may be relieved you're not crazy to go this way.

Off-trail work in timber is possible, but a little more tedious, hopping deadfall and without distant visibility. Be safe when log jumping. More than once have I forgotten how useless boot tread becomes on slippery bark-less trunks. I've escaped uninjured after slipping off smooth logs, nearly being critically impaled by broken branches pointing upward toward my core.

A drippy solo tent on an overcast day in the Cascade Range of Oregon.

Thicker forests outside of the Rocky Mountains are not as welcoming to off-trail travel. The moist mountains of the Pacific Northwest are unmatched in their unique beauty. Coniferous rainforests host tall timber species that battle for sparse sunlight at the top of the forest canopy. It's dizzying to appreciate; it makes you feel small and safe. These steep slopes have woven tapestries of trails to explore, often using expired logging roads that follow contour lines. But beware the bushwhacker. Punching through these fern-floored forests is slow and soggy. Bearings have to come from compasses and GPS receivers as distant ridgelines and landmarks are obscured.

When your confidence in your ability to navigate without a trail increases, you'll seek out the right places, knowing you'll more likely have it to yourself or with a select circle of adventurers who have also broken from the masses. Tread lightly so others can experience the same pioneering spirit.

CHAPTER 6
TIME ON TRAILS

After hundreds of miles on rocky and rooted trails, I've come to appreciate that foot placement matters. Novice hikers, especially youth, seem drawn to the game of stepping on rocks. I, too, did it for years. Don't flippantly play "the floor is lava" along the trail. It's instinctual and gives a false impression of ease.

Instead, think like cross-country runners. They know the surface you stride on matters. The right shock absorption from the ground helps them go further. Experienced long-distance runners intentionally use the edge of asphalt roads rather than adjacent concrete sidewalks inches away; asphalt is a softer surface and slightly absorbs a portion of the joint-jarring impact—at least more than concrete. Dirt does the same, but better. Earth is even more forgiving than warm asphalt. The more you choose to step on soil, the more your legs will thank you.

Foot arches and ankles are unnecessarily strained when perched on top of rocks. The body is forced to repeatedly counter-balance and compensate to not torque the ankle or bruise the arch. Sensibility says to use stones as stairs for climbing, descending, or when unavoidable. Otherwise, move like a snake as you gracefully navigate through a trail that is a mix of soil and stone. Go between the big rocks—not over.

Reducing unnecessary wear on your upper leg muscles is another benefit of this sensible strategy. Each time you step over, rather than around, rocks, you're increasing quad fatigue. The motion of bringing the knee up and down repeatedly could be alleviated by swinging your shoe around. Just as hiking in heavier boots unwittingly increases leg fatigue, so does each vertical quad compression.

These subtle considerations shouldn't slow you down. Allowing them to pause or stutter your stride would be counterproductive. They will become a natural part of your gait with practice as you're watching out for your body. Just as you already avoid treading on injury-causing hazards, you can start stepping for efficiency.

Selecting the softer ground may seem an innocuous concern but remember the long-distance athlete—that's what you are. Backpacking is an athletic event. It is a sport over distance. After thousands of steps per day and dozens of miles, your feet will thank you as they spend more time on the soft, flat ground where the whole foot can bear your pack's weight, and more shock can be sent underground.

Physical Conditioning

I'm convinced that if anxious backpackers concerned themselves more with proper physical conditioning than analyzing gear, there would be far fewer early exits. Such route shortfalls, plan alterations, and all-out cancellations are far more common from someone in the group gassing out than a hiker not having a warm enough down jacket or ideal footwear. A physically fit hiker can more comfortably make do despite mediocre gear or a slightly heavier pack than the out-of-shape. We tend to be more interested in spending the dollars and running the errands needed to lighten our equipment by the ounce; we rarely want to march up hills or hit the stair machine to prepare. If I could choose only one, I'd select hiking alongside a fit backpacking buddy whose legs and lungs are acclimated to incline but whose pack is heftier than recommended. They will likely work it out. Their strength will make up for the gear disadvantage. The opposite does not work as well—that is, a lightweight pack on the physically unprepared. Just like in sports, the shoes don't make the player.

Physically fit people can comfortably walk a few miles without warning, and walking is a great way to stay in shape. That truth is one of the traps that will keep them from proper prep. New hikers hear route distances and shrug them off as doable. After all, our wrist-worn fitness trackers are notifying us of the miles we've stepped each day. They hear the first day will be five or eight miles. Then in their head, they think, "I can do that. That's only a two- to three-hour walk." That may be true on a gentle trail or around the neighborhood, but backpacking is more than walking. It's what I call *complicated walking*.

There are abundant tools available for indoor and outdoor training. Whether you choose a treadmill or the local hills, you'll be better off. But don't be deceived by running or cardio alone. These certainly help your lungs and heart but running uses a different set of muscles than complicated walking (aka backpacking). I've convinced myself that running a few miles or full-court basketball are great ways to stay in shape for the next adventure. But on day two, my hamstrings, hip flexors, and upper quads remind me I did the wrong prep. Nothing beats walking uphill on a trail to train your body for walking uphill on a trail.

The mechanics of walking involve nearly locking your knee each step. As one leg steps forward, the other straightens, briefly stretches the upper quad, and extends the hamstring through the calf muscle in a way that cannot be mimicked by running. They share some muscle groups, but not all. Hiking uphill, especially on a trail, engages the foot, ankle, and Achilles heel uniquely. If you don't have access to an outdoor route with an incline or are limited to walking around your neighborhood, try using the parking strip. The uneven surface of grass adds beneficial tension to your ankles and will toughen them to react over crumbling gravel. You'll look a little odd not using the sidewalk and may make a curious neighbor do a double-take but wait until they see you do it next week donning a full pack! Then the inquiries start rolling in.

If roadside, find dirt roads or walk on the gravel edge, even if it has a side slope. Any uneven surface that challenges your legs more than smooth concrete or asphalt will pay dividends. In a gym, crank up the incline on the treadmill or stair machine.

When you're ready to do more than walking, which you can't do too much, add squats or weights to your training, both train the frame for pumping up an incline wearing extra pounds.

Backpacking trails are rarely smooth nor level—quite the opposite. They are complicated with crumbling gravel, large rocks, protruding roots, soft sand, water runoff, mud mires, snow patches, deadfall detours, and horse manure minefields. At higher elevations, they disappear into ankle-challenging scree fields, bushwhack work, and technical talus slopes. These organic complications slowly erode leg strength over miles. Joint fatigue comes quicker. Each alteration from the body's natural stride—shifting to stabilize an ankle on lose ground or lifting the knee a bit higher over a root—adds unexpected exercise. You can seldomly expect to open your stride and enjoy your natural gait.

Instead, plan on picking your way through wet conditions mixed with trip hazards. These hurdles are also a thrill to overcome. The sense of achievement after challenging rugged conditions over miles is addictive. Your feet will be fatigued, but you'll quietly crave what the next day holds.

Trails frequently become water runoff paths making slippery conditions.

Speaking of the next day, day two is the second surprise challenge that catches the amateur off-guard. Not only are you navigating irregular trail conditions plus toting a pack that has (hopefully) been reduced by pragmatic scrutiny, but you'll be hitting the repeat button tomorrow.

Anyone can over-exert themselves on one day with intense exercise. They know they'll be a little stiff tomorrow, and it will work itself out. But the best backcountry basins are a two-day hike to behold. Taking the second day off to nurse tender muscles and recover isn't the best use of your preparations. First days are filled with vertical as you gain altitude into the range. Second days frequently include switchbacks that carve up 1,000-foot passes and reveal neighboring drainages. The body primed for that initial incline will still wake up a little stiff but will be ready to power through another section.

It's okay to be a bit sore. It's impossible to faultlessly prepare for complicated trail conditions and the precise elevation gain, but you can get close. And getting close in preparedness is what separates the comfortable from the constrained come day two and beyond.

Your physical preparation goal is to pop out of your sleeping bag on day two and, after a long stretch and brief complaint about a small sore spot, be ready to tackle more terrain. As discussed earlier, the first day is frequently the biggest obstacle to overcome. It involves the most elevation gain, the more significant oxygen adjustment to a higher altitude, the heftiest pack of the week with the most food, and overcoming any chafing from straps or clothing. Each day following, your lungs become more acclimated, you're consuming your food weight, your legs feel more powerful, and your gear adjustments are diminished. You're at cruising altitude. Enjoy the flight.

Dropping Personal Pounds

Appreciate the challenge of physical preparation. It will extend your lifespan as you strengthen your legs and lungs. A looming trek can serve as a trigger toward a reasonable weight-loss goal. Each pound shed from your frame is as good or better than a pound shed from your pack. Like physical conditioning, if you had to choose one, it's safer and more enjoyable to explore having reduced a belly by ten pounds than a pack. The prior takes action and lifestyle modifications; the latter is solved with spending.

As you toil tediously to shed five or ten pounds from your gear, consider means to abandon the same weight (or more!) from your body. Weight loss is less expensive, more rewarding, and longer lasting than having fewer pounds on your shoulders for a few days. Enjoy physical weight loss all day, every day. Easier said than done, I know.

Standing shirtless in front of my master bathroom sink was embarrassing. My reflection was pasty, fluffy, and unshaped. I felt observably weak. A desk-job "dad bod" may look healthy on some, but not me. I set a goal not necessarily to lose weight, but to get strong. I acquired a set of high-intensity interval training videos as outdoor workouts were impractical headed into December. Pacific Northwest winters aren't just cold and wet; they're depressingly dark. The extreme course called for 45-60 minutes a day, six days a week for nine weeks. Sweat soaked the 5'x7' area rug in our front office each evening after the kids were in bed. Not a day was skipped—undoubtedly the most physically challenging experience of my life.

Halfway through, I was hitting a wall without adequate protein to recover my muscles within 24 hours. Disdain for protein shakes sent me toward learning how to eat more plant proteins. I dropped thirty pounds over the next six months and settled into three workouts per week and far fewer cheeseburgers.

Months later, I comfortably hammered out a few treks, including an epic ten-day expedition in Wyoming. I can't imagine completing this grueling off-trail circuit carrying a preverbal 30-pound flour bag on my stomach in addition to my gear.

No matter your number, your needs, or your resources, you can get physically prepped enough to experience ear-popping altitudes.

River Rage

Jealousy. Whenever I see someone crossing a river on horseback, I feel it. Such majesty! River crossings, or fords, while horseback are exhilarating and easy-going. The horse marches through on four muscle-bound legs bred for stability. At most, a refreshing splash sprinkles your legs, but you generally stay high and dry. For backpackers, however, rivers equal obstacles. Ice-cold fresh snowmelt is rushing over slimy stones, ready to offer a refreshing break or risking a trip-ending injury.

I've enjoyed wading in water since a neighbor took me under his wing and taught me the quiet art of fly-fishing. This led to a life-long obsession with all things moving water, including eight summers spent river guiding on the Snake River in Wyoming. Even today, when it's time for a break on a day casting up a trout stream, I'm careful to sit where my legs can still feel the pulse of rushing water, even if through waders. Rivers are hypnotic and have my heart.

My experience standing in rivers and staying stable enough to tie a knot while currents rush between my legs gives me the confidence to wade deeper than other backpackers are comfortable. A tall frame doesn't hurt either. But it doesn't always work.

After dropping into a deep canyon's worth of switchbacks, I once encountered a raging river I couldn't cross. The other side held a hidden lake. After scanning the whitewater for weak spots, I deduced the only way across was the shallow tail-out of a glacial lake right before it picked up steam and tumbled away. This wouldn't just require removing boots, but the entire bottom half of my outfit. After ensuring I had privacy, I stripped down and took an unexpected midday half-bath. A few steps to the left and the lake would start moving more like a deep canal and less like stillwater. A few steps to the right were swimming depths. My shirttail and pack bottom dipped into the lake surface as I tiptoed through the gravel to the opposite forest. Dry clothes were spared for the remainder of the adventure. Upon my return, I was fortunate to find a more reasonable river crossing below a waterfall.

The wide tailout of a raging cascade pool offers a primitive ford.

This experiment taught me a lesson for future fords. When you fear roaring rapids may roll your ankle—or your entire frame—look toward the shallow outlet or inlet of a lake as the safer place to cross. Rivers regularly fan wide into deltas at the head of calm lakes. You may end up splashing through a few smaller channels instead of getting wet only once and may stay wet a bit longer, but the face-plant risk factor drops considerably.

Once, I was on the last leg of a weeklong journey and enjoyed conveniently placed logs at each ford to that point. Smaller streams that earlier would flow heavy had turned to harmless hopscotch creeks as the dry August was nearing to a close. One of the advantages of late summer treks is how rivers have calmed themselves. The trade-off: you miss half the wildflowers.

Although I was prepared to ford in my Walmart foam slip-on shoes, I never had the need to switch to the stylish kicks for a knee-deep traverse. As you descend into valley bottoms toward trailheads, the likelihood of encountering raging rivers increases, especially in the early summer, and that is what I encountered that afternoon. Gone are the small feeder streams that collect at high elevations.

There are two river passage possibilities at lower elevations: a rare backwoods bridge has been constructed for hiker safety and livestock demand, or a refreshing ford awaits. The latter is far more common. I can't decide which I prefer but have been glad to see a few backcountry bridges even when they break up the otherwise-pure wilderness, especially when I can *hear* the river before I see it. The sound is haunting as you approach.

The last river I needed to cross was wide, shallow, and slow. I welcomed a break and enjoyed the cool water. As I was drying my feet and lacing up on the opposing shore, two hikers approached from the opposite direction. They didn't pause or strategize their path across. Instead, they splashed forward with high-top, waterproof, leather boots. Each step submerged over the boot height. I cringed. They were early in their expedition and hiking into the hills for who knows how long. Waterproof boots are pointless when water is poured in from the top. It's best kept below half the boot height.

Didn't they know this?

I couldn't imagine how long their newly submerged boots would take to dry in the coming days, let alone the immediate discomfort of hiking in fish tanks. It was painful to witness.

The first step of a crossing is the most breathtaking— literally. The near-frozen liquid saturates whatever you're wearing, stings your swollen skin, and contracts your lungs. Your feet were warm and sweaty a few seconds ago. Now numbness and loss of muscle agility is only a matter of minutes away. The longer it takes to step through the riverbed, the higher your chances of injury. Gracefulness goes after limbs get cold. The clock's ticking, but haste makes waste. Be deliberate but not hurried.

No matter your approach, keep your toes angled upstream. This creates a more streamlined profile to pierce through the pressure. Even when moving your feet, keep them pointed upstream submarine-style. The current can help your stance as it drives your footing toward the rocky streambed. A sideways stance increases drag and risks one leg getting spread downstream. Between each move, ensure one foot is well wedged, preferably between rocks, before your next step. Never step on big submerged stones. Their mossy tops are slick and precarious.

Keep your body weight forward, meaning lean upstream. Lean into the current. If you fall, err forward, so your hands can catch your weight. If you're going to stumble, better to go face first and upstream than allow your backpack to pull you downstream. Falling backward accelerated by backpack weight is unsettling and treacherous.

Lock arms with your buddy when it gets knee-deep or higher. If you have petite people in your group, position them immediately downstream of the more sure-footed. This creates a temporary triangular back-eddy breaking the pressure for the second hiker. Look for boulders that break the current and wade just behind them in their backwater. Trout love to tuck into this refuge from strong currents, as should you.

Aaron demonstrates that one crossing log is helpful—two is better.

If using a log to cross, don't dilly. Spend as little time as possible using as few footsteps as possible. Logs are super for staying dry but hellacious for the hesitant. Just like roller-skating, you're more likely to fall down, or backward, the slower you roll. Use physics to your advantage.

Contrary to natural instincts, motion increases balance. Keep forward momentum so if you trip, you fall toward the opposite shore, rather than down into the drink. Never stop or lean backward on a log, especially while carrying a backpack.

Beware the darker wet sections of half-sunken logs, where whitewater is splashing it. There you will find the slickest surface on Earth. Don't trust it. Always look for rocks and logs with dry tops and rough surfaces where your rubber lugs can ensure grip.

Ford Footwear

The standard approach to river crossings is to switch boots out for a synthetic river shoe, slip-on or laced, that can dry quickly, offer some grip on mossy rocks, and protect the toes. Old running shoes work if you don't care about ruining them in silt. The drawback: running shoe fabrics absorb water and drip all over your pack afterward. They also cannot double as cozy camp shoes once soggy.

Some go the open-toed sandal route. The risk is cramming a toenail between rocks, breaking one of a few backcountry rules to protect your head and feet. You'll need those toes a few more miles. Proceed with caution.

Even more minimal is the socks-only or barefoot approach. I've gone this route a handful of times when the river bottom looks tame. There's something primitive and therapeutic about allowing silt to ooze between your toes. And if you opt to keep your socks on, they offer a somewhat secure stick to mossy cobble, similar to felt-soled wading boots, minus the protection.

The most common answer is foam clog-type sandals. They are ultralight, ultra-durable, and have a protective toe box. They also dry in minutes, ready to pamper your tired toes around camp, with or without socks. The drawback is bulk. Their durability decreases packability. Strap them to the pack exterior but use caution to run the straps *through* the sandal, not just around. Each summer, someone in the group deals with a potential escape artist camp shoe trying to slip off a pack.

After reading several posts from renowned thru-hiker Andrew Skurka, I reconsidered my footwear system this last season. He's written several articles about the disadvantages of must-have waterproof boots, such as *"Why Waterproof Shoes Will Not Keep Your Feet Dry."* Skurka contends that the waterproof layers in boots fail with saturation in moist meadow cover or prolonged precipitation and become breathability detriments. His unorthodox "hike wet" recommendation is a significant paradigm shift for me and the footwear industry. It caught my attention. In short, he recommends embracing the wet, wearing a quick-dry mesh trail-runner, marching right through rivers, and swapping socks regularly. Then before bed, if your feet are macerated, treat with a salve and wake up to healed skin.

Save yourself carrying the weight and bulk of a second pair. Save yourself the time of switching shoes each crossing. And save yourself from cook-drying impossibly immersed leather by fire.

As the majority of the footwear industry communicates, I've been sure that waterproof boots are the end-all-be-all for decades. But I gave this hike-wet system a try this summer over five treks totaling 135 miles. One trip included braving day-long deluges and enduring eight miles of mud puddles. Other trails were bone dry. The synthetic meshy shoes dried swiftly as promised and switching well-designed wool socks prolonged comfort. I never felt too cold nor too wet. The hot days were far more comfortable with increased breathability and nominal perspiration. More dusty grit got between toes than I would prefer but was easy to rinse before bed.

I made one adaptation that increased dry time after fords by taking a moment to remove—rather than ring out—my foam insole. It still caused me to stop and relace at each shore, but I'm not in a race. The verdict: I'm a believer in hiking in wet in quick-drying synthetics. I've dropped foam creek-crossing shoes off my packing list. My high-top waterproof boots might be henceforth limited to shoveling the driveway.

Summer Snow

"Snowball fight!" The crunchy white stuff feels amazing balled in a hot hand. A contrast of temperature, texture, and color creates a welcomed break under bluebird skies in mid-summer. There's something special about encountering a snowfield and starting a spontaneous snowball fight on a warm August afternoon. It breaks the script and reminds the hiker they are somewhere special, somewhere that stays cool and is shaded enough to retain snow year-round.

Snow can also present problems. If you're planning an early summer trek, watch online snowpack-monitoring sites. A phone call to nearby towns can share current trail conditions. Depending on your destination, with one high-pressure system, the report can improve over a few days. Lower-level snowpack—below 10,500 feet—tends to shed quickly when a high-pressure system settles in. Rivers flush, and thawed meadows open the gates to simpler high-country travel.

Lingering summer snow results from one of two seasonal weather patterns: a heavy winter followed by a mild spring or an average winter followed by an unusually cold or wet spring. The calendar-busting worst-case scenario is a wild winter followed by a cold-soaked spring. When this combo occurs, slushy snow and flooded fords can box out the alpine backcountry into mid-July. Each spring is different, but trailheads open from south to north one high-pressure pattern at a time, starting in lower latitudes—range by range and state by state.

Smiling through unexpected conditions, Aaron postholes deep into summer snow.

A decade ago, some friends and I planned an early journey the week of the Fourth of July. We knew it was a risky week to count on in the Rocky Mountain backcountry as it's either the first week trails break open or the last week snow impedes progress. We didn't do the required research and trusted our gut. We were wrong.

At mile four of fifty, we were post-holing thigh-high on level ground below the timberline. The lodgepole pines created generous shadows and retained the heavy winter into early summer. I fatigued and found a place to rest my drenched legs on a sunny granite outcropping. It was time to come to grips with reality. If the snow was this deep in the low country, the snowpack would only get deeper the higher we climbed. Sure, the snow may firm up with altitude, but the expected ford at the nine-mile mark would be raging, and the 12,000-foot pass on day two would be arctic. The three of us had the week off, and the vacation seemed a heartbreaking bust after a few hours. We opted to behave like migrating animals and fly south toward a range 200 miles away. It was the right decision. The trail conditions were wet but passable. Lessening the latitude made the difference as this range was a week ahead in the runoff process.

Above 10,500 feet, there are occasions when stable snowfields increase travel speed as you glide or glissade over otherwise tedious talus fields. The rocky and muddy earth changes to a smooth, white, slanted sidewalk. Advantageous snow is found early in the morning and at higher elevations before sunlight softens the surface. If you're aiming to leverage snowfields as an off-trail advantage, get up early. Afternoons are slushy and can be dangerous once the sun gets to work. However, pitch is paramount. Danger depends on angle.

My son, Jared, was on his second 50-miler as a 13-year-old. We had crossed soft snowfields before, but never this slanted. The rocky trail disappeared under the steep white slab. Black boulders threatened from its base. I tested my tread by kicking a few footprints. Conditions were dicey as the morning shade glazed the surface with an icy crust. Between the pitch, the rocky bottom, and the hardened surface, I proceeded forward against my better judgment. My veteran balance and intentional steps made it across. I justified leading out, thinking my demonstration and fresh footholds would create safer steps for the small group. But a few steps into the crossing, Jared's foothold detached, and his body plunged downward into a slide with no ability to stop.

It all happened fast for him, but for me, it felt like slow motion. There is no more helpless feeling than watching your child fall into certain injury or death. I stood helplessly yelling worthless directions and wincing. My mind raced through worst-case scenarios.

Am I going to watch him die?

He flailed his arms and legs to dig into the ice without success. His body spun on impact of the first boulder then broad-sided the next.

He was alive.

I dropped my pack and leaped down the 100-foot slope after him. The damage assessment: shock, gashed rib cage, lacerated wrist and hand, and leg bruises. Had his head struck first, it would have been much worse.

Crampons could've prevented this danger, but the route didn't call for them. We thought the fields would be milder, less angled, or more open to traction.

When crossing angled snowfields, approach from as low as possible. Never cross when the angle is an arch, curving steeper as it drops. A slide here only gets worse as you descend. Consider what's immediately below—a drop into an icy lake, a boulder field, or an open meadow. Conversely, enjoy crossing when it's concave—flattening as it pans out. These are inviting to glissade sitting atop garbage bags or rain pants.

The center mass of the snow is the most stable. Use caution toward the edges as they melt from the outside inward. Heat radiates from warm border boulders and creates unseen caverns underfoot—a post-hole risk. Give a wide berth to dark rocks that puncture the surface in the middle of a snowfield as they soften their surroundings with radiant heat.

Punching down thigh-high into a snowfield is a concern not only because it's awkward or wet but because it's a severe injury risk. Your foot rockets through into an unseen air cavern below toward sharp boulders ready to sprain ankles and gash chins. Lodged footwear is also probable. Stomping a footprint before giving it your full weight slows progress but reduces risk and increases traction.

Enjoying the payoff of vertical—a gentle glissade off a high pass at 11,000 ft.

If you read contour lines closely and hit the right time of day, the conditions can line up favorably. Crossings and glissades become a welcomed break from the ordinary.

On day five of another trek, I planned a ridge traverse that navigated across a few small glaciers and popped over a 13,300-foot domed summit. From studying the topographic map, it appeared that still-moving glaciers had nearly-level top halves to scurry across, and the east slope looked like the glissade of a lifetime to make a speedy descent. Checking online satellite imagery confirmed my hope. Not only was it a long, safe glissade, but the bottom appeared to pan out to flat snow offering a safe landing if the slip-n-slide ever got severe. There were no boulder islands nor immediate dangers.

Once I reached the summit, I realized I had never been so high in altitude and felt so little wind. It was otherworldly calm. Low clouds clipped the higher peaks, but my 360-degree view was unobstructed. The previous night's cold front dusted the range with two inches of snow, making each boulder resemble Frosted Mini-Wheats cereal. I sat cross-legged on a flat, dry stone to stretch my hamstrings. My dog curled in my lap to borrow body heat. It was one of those conflicting moments when your athletic achievement keeps you warm, but your moist brow and back begin cooling the longer you linger. When I tore myself from my perfect perch on the Continental Divide, I got my first glimpse of that afternoon's entertainment—an 800-foot snow slide. A pair of rain pants turned my rear into racing mode. My boot heels would spray my face full of summer snow each time I wanted to hit the brakes. Climbing the equivalent elevation took me nearly an hour to slowly navigate over wet and lichen-covered talus. The drop took only minutes.

Weather Watch

Backpackers have a special relationship with the sky. Looking skyward in the backcountry is simultaneously inspirational, beautiful, impressive, educational, and concerning. It requires respect and reaction. It demands you know how to balance your behavior between being carefully concerned or dismissive. Weather respect comes from logging hours enduring hail, heat, or high winds. But a pragmatic approach seeks out the common tell-tale patterns of predictability.

My dad taught me to look to the western horizon where the Jet Stream typically ushers in afternoon cloud cover and watch for "thunder bumpers." Later in life, I kept calling thunderstorms "thunder bumpers" until a few people started looking at me funny, having never heard that term before. It must've been generational. Dad would also mark breezes on his watch, celebrating each afternoon wind that cooled his sweaty cotton shirt. At dusk, he'd warn my brother and me, "It gets dark quick out here."

In retrospect, I suppose that was his way of helping us get ready and not to get caught fumbling around in the dark without our D-battery flashlights. But scientifically speaking, it gets dark the latest in the summer, and dusk is the most prolonged. Love you regardless, Dad.

Overly concerning yourself with fear of the next weather event can ruin a voyage. Conversely, not giving the sky its due respect can place you in harm's way. It's impossible to document or discuss all weather patterns seen across various regions, ecosystems, elevations, and seasons. Those who trek in the shoulder seasons, deserts, coniferous rainforests, or low country will need to make appropriate precipitation and temperature adjustments.

Weather watching is essential because your trek exists in full exposure to the elements—man versus nature. Being inside a tent is as weatherproof you can be but isn't all that fun or breathtaking. It's also prudent to know the realistic waterproof limit of your rain jacket or the breathability of your hot weather hiking shirt. Harsh weather—hot or cold—is the ultimate test of promised gear performance and the inner wherewithal required to pass through it.

Thunder Bumpers

My college summers were spent guiding paddle rafts down the Snake River. I call them "golden years" as I reflect on one reason to return to the job—the tan. It wasn't much for pay, but it taught unintended lessons on full weather exposure. Marching through mountains fully dressed with a week's worth of quality gear strapped to your back is much more comforting than paddling downstream toward a darkening thunderhead while armed with a mere set of sandals and a swimsuit—which I did often, and often with inexperienced tourists in my raft. When walls of sheet rain would carve patterns in the surface of the river, you could anticipate the blast as it marked its path. Sun-warmed skin would sting with the first cold raindrops. Then body temperatures would drop as the wind cooled the newly wet and nearly naked bodies on the raft.

As the guide perched on the stern, the command I barked during downpours was "all forward" directing all paddlers to stroke forward in unison. This ensured our progress downstream head-on through the upwind blast, but generally, it helped keep the group's blood pumping. A rapid heart rate is the best warming system ever created. Tourists would eventually tire of paddling endlessly, and their focus would instinctively key on the inclement weather after a rest. Complaints were inevitable. They would turn their head backward toward me to seek validation and gauge if I was equally bothered by the rain. I learned that if I pretended to ignore the rain, knowing it was likely short-lived, their perception would mirror. When they saw me unbothered, they assumed the same attitude. Their grievances would soften to shrugs. Sometimes I would make a point of it by sarcastically inspecting the surface of my forearm through my dripping sunglasses and proclaim, "You're right, it *is* raining. All forward!"

This same type of grit is helpful on the trail. Marching through miles of rain only to saturate your gear isn't wise, but getting comfortable with operating inside a storm, suitably protected, takes not only physical toughness but a learned mental toughness. As with river trips in cold weather, marching onward might be just the right approach to keep warm if you can stay dry. Weather preparedness will prolong your plan and prevent early exits. Similarly, knowing when it's best to duck for cover under thick branches or dive under the tent fly is also prudent.

As Kenny Rogers says, "You've got to know when to hold 'em, know when to fold 'em."

Pragmaticism protects my ego from worrying if I'm too quick to hit pause and watch a storm pass from under a tree. It's a sensible choice. Bouts of "liquid sunshine," as they call it in the Pacific Northwest, are no time for a tough-guy contest. Using natural or tent cover extends your raingear's life for when you may need it later if fully exposed. Thunderstorms at higher altitudes seldom linger more than an hour. In decades of travel, I've only endured hours-long storms a handful of times. Ninety percent of alpine storms last twenty to forty minutes. Reserve your rain gear for operating in that ten percent. Otherwise, save your outerwear. Sit back and enjoy the show.

Witnessing a wild storm roll through a region is a sensory spectacle. It delivers a dazzling show, including flashes from lightning and clouds casting fast-moving shadows. It has waves of foreboding darkness as tall thunderheads give the illusion of midday dusk. Wind causes trees to howl as they sway, thunder shakes the earth, hail bounces off the forest floor, and rain refreshes each plant. Something's got to keep everything so green up there!

During the storm, hold still and watch the direction of the traveling clouds. Once you've pegged the oncoming trend, observe the horizon. That's your forecast.

Afternoon cumulus clouds warn of storms but dazzle as they segment sunbeams.

Lighter gray clouds indicate a broken storm. Breaks of blue sky give hope. If you can see separate clouds, it won't be long. If the entire atmosphere is one uniform color of gray, buckle in—you're in for a few hours. Observe the bottom altitude of the clouds. If you can still see the highest peaks, the storm will be shorter and less severe. The higher the cloud bases, the more you'll only endure rain leftovers as the precipitation has to travel further to hit the ground. Conversely, if clouds sink downward and obscure the upper half of the peaks, that's a storm to respect.

Give your rain jacket and tent fly the occasional shake to shed droplets. It shortens the dry time and reduces fabric permeation. Use care not to drench your boots when dancing with wet tents. When the rain lets up, keep your rain gear and hood on for a while. Your body heat will cook it from the inside for a speedier dry. The wind will take care of the outside. Besides, the air after showers is predictably chilly. And branches and underbrush are waiting to shed their soak on you until they're dry themselves.

Where Water Starts

Partaking of frigid and clear spring water is one of the glorious spoils of voyages in the mountains. I call it "free water" as it requires no work, no pumping, no chemicals, and has no monthly bill. You can fill your belly and tank up to your heart's content. It's year-round outdoor plumbing perfection kept at molar-chilling temperatures without ice. I love finding a spring and walking to its source, imagining the veins underground that come together to create this feature.

Wild water innocence was lost in the early 1980s as outdoor recreationists became increasingly aware of microscopic contamination. Gear companies responded with several filtration and chemical solutions. Pumps and pills became required packing list recommendations. I was educated to guard against all outdoor water and the threat of giardiasis.

My worst experience as a young hiker happened when I naively drank from a small creek near my home, then walked upstream a few more yards only to discover a half-submerged decomposing mule deer carcass. I was mortified. I brushed my teeth vigorously at home, thinking that would help. Fortunately, I didn't get sick.

As a teenager, annual 50-milers were the outdoor classroom where I was schooled to boil or filter every tumbling trickle out of fear that an elk or sheep herd may have deposited disease-laden feces uphill. Protozoa could seep into any spring our group hoped to use. In retrospect, I question the scientific accuracy of that level of through-ground seepage and the likelihood of transmission by proximity.

Even after hearing this doctrine for decades, I admittedly trust natural water sources more than I probably should despite having endured the worst possible outcome—but not while backpacking.

A decade ago, my brother-in-law and I both contracted the same parasite from the same swim-diaper-laden public pool. We spent the day enjoying the crowds with our small families, but as we were leaving, we heard the lifeguards had to close the pool down for a few hours to remove someone's "accident" and sanitize the water. He and I were glad to have dried off before this incident. However, we didn't escape contamination. We both spent the next eight days at home sick and never more than a few hurried steps away from a toilet. I lost nine pounds. He lost twelve. We don't know if we contracted cryptosporidiosis or giardiasis, but it was horrible regardless. The symptoms are painful. The cramping is crippling.

As a river guide, I would occasionally run parched while paddling on scorching summer afternoons. Desperate times called for dipping a Nalgene bottle neck-deep in the drink and gulping a belly full of the sage green Snake. Other times while backpacking, I've enjoyed a lovely looking "spring" only to follow it uphill to discover its source—a mosquito-infested stagnant pond. A glance at my map would've prevented this surprise as detailed topo maps help you trace the origin of small streams.

And still, despite these encounters, I've been reckless more times than I'm willing to admit with water purification and fortunately came out unscathed. Not filtering is a health and safety gamble. It won't always fall in your favor. Don't roll the diarrhea dice as you weigh the inconvenience of treatment against the instant gratification of quenching thirst. Use prudence and err on the side of safety.

There remains a great debate of what we should be more cautionary toward: potentially fecal-contaminated water or poor personal hygiene. Both are wise to watch. We know protozoa and parasites are sourced from fecal matter, but let's be honest: the most likely origin of any poop particles encountered while hiking is from your own body or—even grosser—transferred from your buddy's. I'm not a scientist, but it speaks to reason that casual instead of careful hygiene is the greater of the two threats of contamination. You are your own worst enemy.

Backpackers have to make adjustments to keep their sanitation on the up-and-up while far from sinks, toilets, soap dispensers, and hand towels. Transfer typically enters the mouth from dirty hands. After covering your cathole, scrub hands with water, soap, and grab some wet sand if needed, then finish with hand sanitizer. I won't cover every hygiene method but would advise all to treat your body as a more significant threat to your health than the water. (Sanitation is discussed later.)

After studying extensively about the likelihood of cysts and other nasties in streams and lakes, it's clear that I'll never be completely confident in what I'm drinking unless I'm standing at the source. As a general rule, it's worth the few minutes it takes to treat. Yes, contamination risk is lower the more remote you go and the farther away from grazing livestock and bathing campers you can wander, but unless you can see it coming out of the ground, treat your water.

Spring Watch

Even with that in mind, you can still entertain the goal of treating water as little as possible—not because of reckless indifference or imagined immunity but to savor pure water from every remarkable source you encounter. As you walk along steep slopes, watch what dribbles across your path and take detours when you hop across seeps. Be amazed at how quickly these trickles are sourced just uphill from trails. I've been on several weeklong routes where copious natural springs or melting snowfields were available each day, and I never once needed to filter.

Use the city water you brought to the trailhead to get up to altitude, then be on the lookout. As you study the topography of your route, you'll start to notice areas with likely sources. As your water runs low, put up your spring water antennae and be on water watch.

Rolling terrain shouldn't catch your interest as a probable water source unless you stumble into a noticeable spring. Instead, be on high alert when the trail runs along the foot of steep slopes. The water dripping out from the foundation of peaks and snowfields is the good stuff. If a stream is large enough to be mapped, don't get as excited. You're looking for the little unmapped trickles with an audible flow. Sometimes a spring will do just that—spring—and tumble only a few yards above ground before soaking back into the soil. It doesn't take much flow to tank up a liter. Investigate upstream toward the sound of it making a drop and you'll find higher cubic feet per second and enjoy a quicker fill.

Springs become reliable at altitude as steep slopes direct summer snowmelt.

Wandering deep in the backcountry near Yellowstone National Park found me empty on water and crossing tributary streams. I could've stopped to filter at the fords, but I kept pushing onward. I was regretting hopping over previous perfect little springs earlier in the day. I should've tanked up then. The dusty trail suddenly turned into a wide mud wallow. Horse hoofs and hiker prints expanded the path as they each suspected the edges would offer stability from the sludge. I tiptoed on the edge of the mud mounds and cringed against an impending misstep. Once across, the thought came to me: "Something is creating this mess."

I turned around and wandered off-trail and uphill around a soggy sloped meadow. At the head of the soft ground and only a dozen yards from the trail, the bog turned to a braided trickle. A few steps more and the braids came together from one spring just wide enough to dip my hydration bladder. It was so cold it gave me a brain freeze. I could barely drink it as it felt chilled to 33 degrees. That near-frozen spring was the source of a giant muddy trail mire below. I camped nearby and enjoyed endless refrigerated refreshment for two days.

When you find that perfect trickle and are confident in the source, it's one thing to dip your bottle and quench your thirst, but it's another to experience drinking it straight from the spring. Take a moment to drop your pack and put nothing between you and the purest water on Earth. Crouch down on your hands and knees and suck with your face in it like an animal. It's primal, exhilarating, and entertaining.

The following broad rules that guide pragmatic water selection aren't scientific but were developed from practical experience. If you can see the source, or the source is from under a steep slope towering above, drench your bottles and savor drinking straight from it. That's why you came! If above the timberline, be even more trusting. Glance at a map and ensure there's not a lake above you where someone could've bathed the week prior. Seek water that when you look above it, you only find contour lines and sky. If you spy water lined with watercress, you can be more trusting of the source. Watercress is an indicator species of natural year-round flow and cannot grow in an intermittent stream sourced from snowmelt.

If it's a small stream, river, or has any lake or pond upstream, treat it. Remember, you're trying to avoid drinking anything someone—or some mammal—could have washed in previously. Try to drink lake water only as a last resort. It's the highest in temperature, the most likely bathwater, bitter-tasting, full of swimming mosquito larvae, and other micro trout snacks. Lastly, if your only choice is a scuzzy pond or turbid river runoff, I've been there. Rig a makeshift prefilter by running your water through a handkerchief to reduce silt and "little swimmers" before you treat it. This extra step will extend the life of your filter cartridges too. It's not a perfect system, but it dramatically cuts down on the crud.

Boiling is impractical, and this book is all about sensibility. It uses fuel or requires excess firewood. It also requires a nice pot and the perfect setup to balance everything. Various pump filters are well designed but are expensive, bulky, and heavy. They utilize combinations of fabric prefilters, carbon, and silver to purify. Newer gravity-driven filters are ideal for larger groups—a great arm-fatigue saver, but impractical for small groups for their size and weight. There are petite squeeze filters you can push or suck the water through. They are compact and lightweight but require much force and clog easily. Iodine pills kill the bad stuff but leave a terrible taste without the taste-neutralizing tablets, largely Vitamin C (ascorbic acid). Covering the taste with flavoring powders also works well. Another drawback: iodine permanently stains plastic bladders and bottles a dingy orange.

After fumbling around with each of these methods and materials' trade-offs, I've settled on using two-part liquid chlorine-dioxide drops almost exclusively. This system checks all the boxes of minimal weight, compact size, affordability, durability, taste, and speed. In just a few minutes, the combined two solutions can treat a liter or two with no fatigue and no risk of mechanical failure. It tastes like culinary city water, much preferred than the odd aftertaste of iodine or saccharine powders.

The Water Conundrum

One of the heaviest items in your pack by volume is water — each liter of the cold stuff tips the scale at 2.2 pounds. Combined with the average hard plastic bottle, which weighs seven to ten ounces, your hydration system can easily be over three pounds. (We will cover bottle and bladder considerations later in the gear chapter.) It's ironic and almost hypocritical for backpackers to tediously care about their pack weight after cautiously selecting various items to reduce the load ounce-by-ounce only to carelessly lug multiple pounds of water for miles "just in case." The water conundrum is complicated and one of the sport's puzzling Catch-22s. It seeks to compare the necessity of preparedness with the advantages of hiking light.

It Hurts on the Outside and Helps on the Inside

When fully loaded with H_2O, you're more prepared to go miles without the worry of crossing another source. You can help others in need or have some to cook a meal later. But beware, carrying water just to *feel* better can be counterproductive. Its weight is slowly sapping your strength and — ironically — causing you to need more as you travel. Water weight is a necessary evil as it can make you *feel* worse.

Conversely, hiking with half as much or just enough saves pounds instantly. Those pounds are spared from being carried over miles — but you expose yourself to dehydration. Transporting less can unwittingly cause you to drink less for fear of running out prematurely. This chain of decisions affects your physical ability to withstand heat, sickness, and all that comes with burning calories without enough water— hence, the conundrum.

I've debated this quandary along the trail with hiking buddies. The consensus is that too many hikers carry unnecessary and heavy amounts of water out of sheer fear of the unknown, of what may not be available up ahead. Their confidence in their chances to find water in the future burdens their pack now, or their annoyance with the purification process adds to the fear of not daring to waste a drop. These amateur thinking errors are based on fear and overcome with preparation, hard-won experience, or both.

Water's cruel irony is that it hurts your body when carried on the outside but helps your body when transferred to the inside. Drinking your water lightens your pack and strengthens your physiology concurrently. Leaving it on your back for later hurts more than it helps—prolonging your pack weight and daring dehydration.

The big question is always, "How much should I carry?" The answer is the classic attorney reply: "It depends." It varies by body type and circumstance.

Drink early and drink often. Down a liter on the bumpy road to the trailhead. Starting fully hydrated allows you to carry a little less without fear of running low too quickly. Slurp generously early in your hike. Remember, it's better for you in your belly than on your back. Peeing it out as you go is better than mustering an extra liter for miles unnecessarily.

Uphill or downhill matters. Drink early into a climb. Avoid carrying much up a pass if there's likely water to fill a bit later. I've rarely ascended a pass without drinking from the mountain on the climb. Trails carved into the low saddles of ridges also happen to run where water collects and leaks out. Hike uphill on a quarter tank or less. Your legs and lungs will thank you. Conversely, near the top or early into your descent, be on water watch for what's tumbling under the talus.

Carry a full tank down from summit springs and snowfield drips into that evening's camp. Your downslope stride won't mind the extra weight as much, and you'll want it at camp later when lake water is the only choice. One of the only times I max out my two-liter bladder is cresting a ridge or powering downhill, or on the rare trailhead beginnings when good water isn't likely for miles on day one. No source can outdo the pure water spilling from high-altitude passes. Be wise that sometimes it's available near the top going up, but not on the backside.

Get it while the getting's good. As you never know what's ahead, don't be embarrassed to change your mind. Several times, I've tanked up on a decent spring only to dump it out and completely refill a hundred yards later at a superior and colder fountain. Sometimes it's because the source looked much higher quality; other times it's because the latter had a heavier flow making the detour efficient.

Study the map. It takes a bit of forecasting, but a plan will reveal how often you're crossing small streams or passing a lake. But beware, some small intermittent streams shown on maps vanish mid-summer. Come August, they're ghosted ravines. When you select your likely source, be patient. The twenty-minute delay it takes to treat is worth not carrying two pounds for a few miles unnecessarily.

Watch your map for drainage direction. For example, when the trail rides along a high ridgeline divide, the grade sends water away from your path. Tank up beforehand. When you can't count on a refill until the first lake at the end of the day, tank up. When your hike involves a hot afternoon, tank up. But with that tank, sip it quickly and pee it for a few miles on near empty. Conversely, if your map shows the trail intersects feeder creeks every mile, don't burden yourself with full tanks.

Hike a mile on empty. It's a little unnerving at first, but it's okay. Remember, your gullet is sloshing with the previous hours of hydration. Be on the lookout, but don't panic. If you're stopping to pee regularly, you're in good shape for a short-term lightweight stroll while you search. My favorite strategy is timing water, so I'm running out halfway up an incline and popping over the top on empty. There's a satisfaction knowing you climbed as light as possible, that the water is in your system, not on your back.

Liters are different for everyone. I regularly hike with a friend who can power through a three-liter hydration system before I finish two. He's roughly the same physical size, but his physiology seems to require more. Be generous with yourself as a novice but keep mental notes of how quickly you're burning through liters. If you're regularly running out or sloshing into camp with loads remaining, adjust accordingly in the future.

Peeing clear isn't the goal. You've heard the axiom that you're not adequately hydrated until you're peeing clear. While it's true you are sure to be well flushed, it could also suggest you're too hydrated. It is possible to have too much water in your system. Excess water negatively affects endurance endeavors as it inadvertently dilutes your blood and lowers your salt and electrolyte levels. If you've been peeing clear for hours, dial down a bit and snack on your salty stuff.

Cairn Confessions

Cairns are found off-trail or where trails fade on tricky terrain. These little stacks of balanced rocks line up like airport runway lights for the weary backpacker to guide their way. Usually, I'm grateful and relieved to know I'm on the right path when I see one. It's a message from the past that whispers, "It's this way."

But in some cases, if I'm being honest, cairns get overused. If you're the person who is building a cairn out of boredom or just because you took a break along the trail and decided to balance rocks while your buddy relaces, please stop. I'm the guy who's kicking them over! If there's a clear trail below a cairn, there shouldn't be a cairn. The trodden footpath is its own marker. Let's minimize our outdoor decor.

Properly placed cairns have spared me more than once. One summer, I had the idea to punch into an unknown basin that was trailless on its last few miles. Intuition told me there had to be a trail. There's no way these lakes have been back there all this time with no use trail to access them. Regardless, I budgeted the time it would take to tediously pick through the timber and work my way up the wooded valley.

Fortunately, three miles into the seven, another solo backpacker crossed my path, heading out along the main trail. We got to talking and exchanged experiences. He shared how he accidentally found a path and knows where it begins. He didn't get to use it on his way in, but he stumbled into it on his way out and had just finished following it out of the basin. I was relieved to hear it would be more comfortable than I planned!

Even with his instructions, the trail's origin was difficult to discover. My steps took me in a crisscrossed grid pattern like a bloodhound trying to pick up a scent. I finally found it. Like most use trails and game trails designed by muscular elk, it had a blatant disregard for human life, charging straight up a timbered incline without an effort to switch back and forth like a maintained human trail. Up I scrambled, cursing its grade but grateful for the regular cairns built on lichen-covered granite boulders to mark the way. This trail was faint and would disappear where tired timber had fallen. But the cairns were dependable, accurate, and regular. I rebuilt a few that had blown over. That route saved me hours on entry and exit. I'll use it again to access the beautiful cirque it hosts and the great fishing it hides.

Recently I was descending an off-trail saddle with a friend. The obvious route was down. All we had to do was follow the trickle of spring water. You could see the target lake below us. But a line of curious cairns ushered us left and diagonally up a slight incline out of the gully as we were dropping toward the tree line. I was trying to go down—not up. I cautiously trusted the cairns' invitation. When back in the gully, we looked backward. Hindsight revealed the steep drop covered in a thick wall of willows and gnarled timber. We would have barreled right into that mess, but bushwhackers before us found the smarter path and took the time to help fellow followers. Their cairns spared us.

The more miles you meander off-trail or on faint trails—which I much prefer to the six-foot-wide dusty arteries near trailheads—the more you'll appreciate cairns when you need them. Use them sparingly to preserve the feel of the last wild places on Earth while still offering an outstretched hand to the weary wanderer. Save them for areas of fallen timber, talus slopes, scree fields, and high tundra. Likewise, join me in the campaign of dismantling superfluous stacks!

Time for a Break

Breaks along the trail have a silly stigma—sneered as failures. Everyone's had a role in this play. Two or more hikers are moving along at what seems like an agreeable pace until one of them exclaims, "Break time!" Others judgmentally roll their eyes at who needs it. The hiker is sweating, panting, and scrambling for an inviting sitting log or boulder, usually the group's least fit. The break feels like a broken rhythm or a dissention from unity. Concerns swirl in others' minds if this will be a problem all day.

Is this person cut out for this trek?

I've been on the judging end of both roles and know how it feels to be the slow one as well as the concerned pacemaker.

The stigma of frequent breaks equating to trip failure is unnecessary. Unless not achieving your distance that day puts you in grave danger of the elements, or you're a thru-hiker racing against seasons or the next re-supply, let it go. Backpacking, like the cliché quote about life, is a journey, not a destination. Traveling down the trail is a significant portion of the entire journey, not a burden to be busted through.

Granted, if your pack is grossly overweight, walking with it strapped to your spine is absolutely a burden. Those totting plus-sized packs would understandably prefer the carrying part of the day end as soon as possible. Heavy loads are a common cause for breaks. When the whole group is wearing them, their desire to get the hiking part over with accelerates. It's a painful irony as heavy packers can't wait until camp when they can drop the load yet require more rest along the way.

Conversely, when packs lighten, the need for breaks decreases and, more importantly, the hiking rush diminishes. Comfort is enjoyed throughout the day, not just when hip belts are unclipped. Breaks aren't failures and can bring unexpected benefits.

For one, breaks reveal wildlife. I've lost count of the number of times quietly pausing to rest in the wilderness has revealed otherwise unseen animals. Backpackers have a nasty habit of tunnel vision. They put up blinders as their sole focus becomes the next step or worse, memorizing the other person's methodic boot heels a few steps in front. No fauna will be seen between you and your hiking partner's tread.

This one-inch toad wouldn't have been spotted without a break along the trail.

Breaks break the script. As you rest, intentionally face a different direction than the trail. Get a glance backward at where you've been. Scan sideways across the canyon you're ascending. That's when the curious ermine will pop up to investigate the commotion, or the screech of a lofty hawk is appreciated. Looking across the meadow will show the cow moose with her two gangly twins. The only times I've seen a herd of backcountry bighorn sheep is when I'm stopped and staring off toward the distance. You'll spot more wildlife seated than bumping the occasional velvet buck from its midday bed.

Breaks promote hydration. If you feel a light headache approaching, you're likely dehydrated. Taking breaks reminds everyone to drink up. Moisture is removed from your body not just from noticeable sweat, but it is also evaporated from your skin in the wind and sun. Just living outside in the elements, regardless of how much you're perspiring, will drain your system quicker than dwelling indoors at room temperature, roofed, and without wind.

Breaks remind you to capture in-the-moment photos. Whip out the camera and fire away—candid or posed. Regardless if you're in a picturesque area, if greeted by another group, don't be ashamed of asking for their help. Procure a quick group pic and return the favor. Do this daily as only a few shots may line up just right. Your favorite backpacking photos years later won't be of single members sitting around camp. They'll be the action photos taken along the trail with packs clipped in. Same for you solo trekkers. Hand your camera over, or all the week's pictures will be awkward selfies and scenery.

Breaks help you be still. Enough can't be said about quiet time. It's called various names—meditation, being in-the-moment, finding tranquility, mindfulness, and silent prayer. Breaks allow you to center your soul. You're away from daily distractions. Campsite chores will beg for your attention later tonight, but at this moment, along this trail, you can be 100% one with yourself and nature. You have a chance to think clearly, do some serious self-reflection, and for believers, commune with your Creator. Take advantage of it. Even if privacy is scarce on a group trek, find some comfortable separation to capture these fleeting moments. It doesn't take long—minutes at most.

When time is up, and it's back to business, get in the habit of walking away backward after you clip in your hip belt. Haste makes waste. Survey the rest stop for dropped lip balm, wrapper corners, sunglasses, or other slippery sundries.

Not doing this one deed caused me to lose three items in one week. I walked away from a camera tripod attached to a branch on day one, a pair of wool socks set on a log on day two, and a wet dog leash drying on a limb on day six. Last year, my haste caused me to unknowingly leave behind my favorite red handkerchief that's been by my side for several hundred miles. Rest in peace, hanky. I'll find you someday!

CHAPTER 7
CAMPSITE CONSIDERATIONS

After miles of wandering in the wilderness, each trekker has a critical and careful decision to make—where to rest tonight. If you're proficient enough to have been there before, or if it's your favorite spot, the labor was done previously. You've worked out the kinks and know where to build. But there's an adventurous spirit about campsite considerations in a new place. For one, you're going to make a home out of next-to-nothing, a few sticks, and stones, a foreign corner of the forest. Others may have been here before and hopefully only left footprints, but for you, you're in pioneer mode.

When you know you're close to the targeted camping area, put down your water antennae and replace them with campsite eyes. Start surveying the land for a few indicators weighing geography, weather, ground, solitude, and proximity.

Walk a radius. Drop your pack in the first spot that comes close to a match to your campsite preferences but be patient. Too many trek leaders rush this part of the plan. Be noncommittal at first. There might be something better. Air out your sweaty back while you enjoy a mild exploratory walkabout. Think of it as a habitat treasure hunt. I've suffered buyers' remorse more than once after setting up at the first welcoming tent site only to discover a superior spot after my camp is literally set in stone. Had I been patient, I could've enjoyed a grander view or better kitchen boulders. I've made my group nervous more than once when they've seen me drop my pack at what appears to be a perfectly decent site only to watch me walk off into the sticks bareback.

"Where are you going?"

"Isn't this where we are camping?"

The answer is always, "Maybe."

Geography is one of the primary factors. Previous chapters address how to size-up slope, gauge advantageous body contours, and generally flat ground. But geography also forecasts the weather, specifically where cold air settles, what direction storms arrive, and where natural wind walls are situated. Settling into the lowest part of the area, usually near lakes and streams, is not only discouraged in Leave No Trace practice and prohibited by regional rules, but it also places your new home where cold air collects. Think of cold air like water pouring into a valley. By sunrise, it fills the container from the bottom upward.

Rather than plopping down in the open meadow bottom, get creative if there are rolling variations in the side slopes uphill. Your cooldown walkabout can reveal subtle and comfortable terraces that perch you slightly above the valley bottom and increase your temperature at sunrise by five to ten degrees. If fog settles in, you'll be above the gray soup. It doesn't take much flat ground to host a tent or two when slopes hesitate. This creativity also provides privacy and elevated vantage points.

If you've been watching the sky, you're savvy to cloud currents in the area. When foul weather rumbles, as it can at any time, look for the "dry side" of tall timber. Rain rarely falls vertically in summer storms. More frequently, it's poured diagonally—hopefully not horizontally—with the wind. In the Rocky Mountains, this is generally from the west. In August, during the more monsoonal season, humid storms rumble in from the southwest. Nesting on the east side of heavy timber doesn't guarantee you won't get wet, but you'll gain a filter rather than enduring the full throttle. It also provides afternoon shade as the sun scorches from the western hemisphere of the sky.

Similar guidelines give you reprieve from wind, an irritating element of weather. Sometimes I'd prefer to set up a tent and cook dinner in a drizzle than relentless wind. Favoring either is up for debate, but wind negatively affects so many aspects of comfort. Vestibules flap loudly, cooking systems struggle, fire-building becomes frantic, skin warmth is ripped away, line casting goes wayward, and sound sleep is interrupted. One benefit: it blasts away menacing mosquitos, who can hardly handle the slightest breeze. But otherwise, I'm not a fan (pun intended). Conversely, though also less-than-ideal, a calm drizzle is dreamy for deep sleep, advantageous for angling, and conifer cover can be regularly located for cooking.

Fortunately, there are strategies to find natural wind walls, even without heavy timber available. Wind works similar to whitewater as it churns across ridges and burrows through gaps. Behind each rock in a river is a back eddy, where currents briefly flow upstream to fill the void. Understanding similar yet invisible air currents reveals calm spots. Each side of a canyon or ridge has a more protected half where consistent winds curl backward and swirl. Rocky terrain can offer the lee of a leaning boulder for breaks. Each lake also has a windy end and a calm end. In the West, where possible, look toward camping on the west side of exposed lake cirques. Your bay will be more tranquil than the splashing shoreline found on the eastern end.

Wherever you've built your home, don't wander off until you're waterproof. You'll need to leave camp to find water, a better view, or for hours of fishing or peak-bagging. Just as you wouldn't go far without water, don't leave camp until you've asked yourself, "If it started raining abruptly right now, is all my stuff okay?"

Tents are zipped, packs are tucked against trunks or stowed under vestibules, and food is unexposed. The only exception is drying laundry. Sometimes I'll just leave it out during a downpour just to give it a fresh rinse.

Each unique campsite creates a memory in your backpacking story.

Then when you're across the lake chasing cruising trout or coming down off a peak after a scramble, and the dark skies gather, you're not worried about your gear. The same rule applies before bed. Never leave camp nor fall asleep without planning on an hour-long deluge rolling through. That way, when awoken at 2 a.m. to rain, you can confidently smile and say, "I knew that was going to happen." Roll over and go back to sleep perfectly prepared.

Good ground is second on my list of priorities. Previously established encampments offer advantages of perfectly positioned log "furniture" or pre-built campfire rings. High-use sites are also preferred for large groups as uncharted ground can frequently only offer one level tent site, but rarely multiple. The trade-off is that heavier-used sites have increased dust and decreased rain absorption.

I rarely sleep in one place for two nights, which helps reduce grief if I'm settling on previously untouched vegetation. It will bounce back in short order with minimal impact. There's a charm in design-your-own, low-usage nooks. However, if you're planning on homesteading for two nights or more, look for established sites to reduce wear and tear.

Previous guests' habits, or lack thereof, are another concern. One strategy is to use well-worn sites for campfires and cooking but set your tent on the sidehill a short skip out of sight. This hybrid approach provides the convenience of a pre-arranged cooking space with reduced unwanted nocturnal visits from bears or "mini bears" like raccoons, squirrels, and other sniffing critters. Opportunistic omnivores get accustomed to what's left behind not just by you but unknown prior guests. You may be by-the-book diligent with food safety and smells, but it's impossible to know the discipline of your predecessors.

Solitude is the unsung secondary advantage of perching on small sidehill terraces. You've walked all this way to get away. Be away! Just a few more steps will increase solitude for you and those who hike through during your stay. Both parties will be none the wiser. I enjoy solo backpacking and group treks, but I lean introspective and introverted in camp, regardless of my group size. I don't mind chit-chat with fellow hikers on the trail, but I'd rather not see, hear, nor feel obligated to strike up small talk with each passerby. I want them to feel like they have the place to themselves and my ignorance is my bliss.

Backcountry angling pays—this cutthroat lives 23 miles from the nearest trailhead.

Proximity to utilities as a campsite criterion can be tricky. The draw toward convenience to water or recreation forms unsightly and unhealthy wilderness wear. It's the cause for campsite distance minimums away from lakes and streams. National forests and wilderness areas can require minimums of 100-200 feet from lakes, trails, and creeks, depending on the region. There will be times when terrain, the abundance of streams, or tight canyons limit choices, and the only hospitable option breaks one of these rules. Please do your best to save these occasions for when it's the only option, a rare exception. That's where map reading comes in. Learning to read topography is similar to looking into the future. Look for slightly larger gaps in between contour lines where the earth flattens for a bit. Here you can spot likely sites away from high traffic and reduce pinch points against water features.

Custom pre-trip cartography can reveal likely extracurricular activities. Your day could include climbing a pitch or scanning the shoreline for rising trout. Select the side of the lake closer to favorable shoreline casting or more likely to host spring water. Proactive planning can place you in ideal campsites that increase enjoyable experiences, provide utility, and still heed Leave No Trace principles.

A campsite's view is frequently bragged about in social media but decreases in importance as you review these more pragmatic principles. Whether you're perched on a secluded sidehill or tucked into a wind-guarded glen, an epic vista is usually only a few steps away. When your meal is warm, or you're sipping a steaming mug, take a short stroll with it in-hand and find an inviting sitting log. There's peace in waiting for piping-hot food to cool while getting lost in a distant gaze or being mesmerized by moving water. Your view is anywhere you can be calm and doesn't have to be where you camp.

Eleven years ago, I was camped with two buddies in the back of an alpine cirque below two large glacier-formed lakes. The outlet creek tumbled down a steep willow-lined canyon below us, and the lake was a short diagonal jaunt uphill to our south. After bumping a bull moose from his afternoon in the willow bottoms, we found the perfect spot up a short steep hike on the canyon wall. It offered the only two places to pitch our gear on a granite shelf jutting out from a steep forested slope. We secured our tents just in time for the pre-dinner hailstorm. Yelling was the only way to communicate during the deafening deluge.

It blew through from the southwest to the north and down the canyon but gave us a break immediately afterward—a chance to step away from our timbered camp to a wet granite outcropping clifftop. We watched as the wall of hail rolled impressively northward. The setting sun clashed orange alpenglow against the cumulus. That perch became our vantage for each meal. It had an ideal granite countertop for cooking plus additional slabs for seating and star gazing. When we had our fill, it was back into the timber for the night. Sometimes the memorable campsites will be unplanned and inconveniently uphill.

Functional Fires

Once camp is staked down and gear is nested, many campers default instinctively toward campfire creation. The campfire is the most prehistoric nighttime activity of humankind and synonymous with camping. It provides evening entertainment with dancing flames. Rising red embers lead the upward eye toward yellow stars. Like moving water, watching fire flicker is hypnotizing and calming. Warm, dry air radiates as it offers a sense of safety and security. Stoking the flame to maintain the right size is a game all its own. And despite the romance and reassurance campfires provide, it's an activity I've wholly omitted from most evenings.

Pragmatically speaking, by the time the skies darken, the backpacker who has hit the trails, climbed cliffs hard all day, or fished into the evening dusk should be seeking to snooze. Rock hopping fatigues the feet, and the miles catch up to you come evening. Living outdoors feels different than at home, where soft seating abounds. Regardless of backpacking in lowlands or high alpine, rests are literally rock-hard, made of wood, or gritty ground. By day's end, the comforting call of a bouncy, insulated pad tucked under your billowy down bag sounds luxurious.

Days are deceivingly long in the summer. The lights are on for more than 15 hours most weeks, especially early in the summer near June's solstice. Robins and squirrels welcome the sunrise before 6 a.m., and headlamps aren't needed until 10 p.m. As much as you may fight it, each day you spend outdoors, your body adjusts to the sun's early-to-bed-early-to-rise schedule.

Furthermore, fishing is ideal right up until darkness overtakes dusk, and sometimes beyond. Some of the best backcountry angling is accomplished by squinting through the last bits of daylight and listening for—rather than seeing—a rising trout's splash. By the time anglers are off the water, there's little time to gather firewood nor energy to maintain a flame, especially when you recall that the unwanted squawking squirrels will sound the sunrise alarm in about seven hours.

When a campfire is needed, it serves a utilitarian purpose and is rarely for relaxation. Some may find that a pragmatic pity. But fires add an optional household chore. And at their worst, they add an avoidable fire hazard to the arid West. They require construction, wood gathering, maintenance, safety, and proper dousing. In the morning, they need to be dispersed and dismantled. View functional fires as a tool within a practical backpacking worldview used only to bake trout, burn bits of trash, or dry soaked socks. On a particularly wet or cold day, it's a recommended respite to thaw bones. On a weeklong solo trip, I may only create one or two fires, and if I do, they are short-lived with minimum lifespans required to achieve the task at hand. For the solo trekker, they are a process. However, if I'm trekking with my teenagers or friends, and the chores are more easily divided among the team, campfires become more beneficial than bothersome.

Practical campfires serve a utilitarian purpose like baking wet fabrics.

Trouble Breaking is Trouble Burning

Another easily preventable eyesore is the partially blackened log found in far too many cold fire rings. Please start and finish sensible fires. Unless you require maintaining a fire for more than a few hours, an essential in extreme weather, avoid using timber that's bigger than your wrist.

You can possess long-lasting and perfectly productive fires constructed entirely of dry sticks no thicker than your thumb. Speaking of thumbs, here's a good rule of thumb: if it's trouble to break, it's trouble to burn. The maximum thickness of firewood that real-world backpackers need is readily snapped over a rock or knee. And be careful with using your knee. Instead, whack it strategically over a sharp boulder's edge or stomp on it. The boulder break may rattle your wrist once in a while, but it won't damage those knees you'll need to hike out.

Avoid the undeniable draw to seek the larger logs. Don't mistake them as more productive or desirable. They're not. Big wood gets only partially burned, but never down to coals nor ashes. The goal is to burn what you start down to bits that disintegrate when scattered, that dissolve in the next deluge. If you can't readily break it, skip it. If you can't burn it down to charcoal, leave it be. Don't leave it partially burned for me.

Keep flames small, sensible, and purposeful. Use common sense by choosing durable ground that can handle heat and heal quickly. Dig up and stash the soil to be replaced in the morning. Select proper wood that's fallen, dead, dry, and requires no cutting. Consider wind safety with rising embers, proximity to flammable gear, and distance from shelters if cooking smellables. Walk a circle around it to remove trip hazards. These tips aren't the entirety of campfire courtesies. Other guidebooks explore endless additional fire-building considerations. Be safe out there.

Leave Only Footprints, Not Fire Rings

The romance of arriving at a textbook campsite comes with mixed emotions when an ash-filled and abandoned campfire ring is discovered. Rocks stained with soot and a partially blackened log left as a centerpiece is an unsightly welcome mat. The pioneering spirit is dashed when wondering if anyone has ever been here before with a clear answer.

"Yes. And they left this to remind you they were here. You're welcome."

In fairness, there have been times when I'm relieved to find a ring in the perfect spot after a long day (if I do decide to make a campfire). But that's the rare exception. The small chore it takes to gather a few stones together and prepare the ground is a small price to pay for the illusion that you're the first person to camp there. The Leave No Trace disciple in me would choose to build something than deal with leftovers.

Campfire rings left constructed are an all-too-common backcountry blight. Recently I returned to one of the first places I backpacked. The trail was composed of less topsoil than I remembered as a teenager. Earth gets worn down to bedrock over decades of dusty traffic. Crews had carved a few new switchbacks along its steeper sections. But otherwise, the mountain hadn't changed much over the years. My nostalgia was dashed when I got to the lake. As I circumnavigated its familiar shoreline, an abandoned fire ring was available every few hundred feet—a few within eyeshot of the next. I dismantled several during my stay, a chore which only takes minutes, but it was discouraging to see evidence of so much usage. I would've rather ignorantly imagined a more pristine place.

That's the beauty of leaving only footprints—those behind you can have similar primitive pioneering impressions unaware it's been done before. This ignorance is bliss.

Ironically, backpackers leave too many fire rings as a supposed favor for the next group. The logic seems sound.

"Surely they'll want this. We will save them the trouble of building and us the trouble of taking it apart."

A win-win, it seems, until the lazy logic is repeated for each group or each campsite.

I'll never forget the Peach Schnapps Altar. After more than a weeklong loop in Wyoming, Aaron and I selected a lake five miles from the trailhead setting us up for an easy exit on the last morning. Upon arrival, we noticed an apparent campsite tucked away from its south shoreline. Multiple tent sites were available, as was a two-foot-tall fire-altar. It may have started as a fire ring, but over the years, and inch-after-inch of neglected ash, it climbed into what could have passed for an Old Testament-worthy sacrificial altar topped with an empty bottle of peach schnapps. I had never seen its equal! Each group who had camped before decided to build on—rather than disperse or bury—the previous ashes. You could see the original ring, now the foundation, with each rock layer stacked to contain the next layer of ash and plenty of foil.

We used it one last time to foil-broil a pair of trout—our burnt offerings on the altar to the fishing gods—but in the morning before our exit, we took the time to get our hands dirty, tossing blackened stones as far apart as possible and carrying several gallon bags of ash in every direction was invigorating. We reduced twenty-some inches of soot to a few. It was impossible to remove it entirely without tools, but we got it down the original circle. It took sand, soap, and lake water to scrub our volunteer firefighter hands clean.

Dismantle More Than You Create

Imagine the scores of once-used campsites that would be transformed if every conscientious camper exited the backcountry with a net-negative campfire ring score as they disassemble more rings than they create. Of course, not every circle needs to be tossed, but you can easily dismantle the superfluous one-time-use ones. High-use altars can be reset. Burnt foil fragments from previous groups are lightweight and can be harmlessly added to your trash bag.

After dismantling a ring by shot-putting its stones and spreading or burying ashes, go the extra mile and bring in handfuls of fresh soil. Use flat rocks or slabs of decaying pine bark as spades. Sprinkle some pine needles and cones. Kick some earth. Toss in an unscarred rock, pine boughs, or deadfall branches. It's like decorating a cake with anything you can grab from the cupboard. Impress your friends with the game of "Can you tell there was a fire here?" Others will never notice your work—and that's the whole idea! This leave-no-trace behavior works well to hide how you heated your home-away-from-home. Similar skills are needed to deal with other utilities, like plumbing.

Toilet Time

We call it that, but it's not accurate. There's a noticeable lack of porcelain in the backwoods. However, in some high-use national park backcountry campsites, pit toilets have been strategically placed in remote areas to consolidate impact. My personal favorite is on the southeast shore of Shoshone Lake, deep in the grizzly country of Yellowstone National

Park. After paddling your canoe across Lewis Lake and portaging it upstream a few miles into Shoshone, you can enjoy not only one of the largest non-motorized backcountry lakes in America but one well-placed rare toilet in the backcountry. A hundred yards from one of the campsites, this seat has no plumbing, outhouse, nor privacy wall. It sits alone atop a pit, perched in a gap in the forest with an open northward lakefront view for your brief stay. You can listen for loons or smile and wave with pants down to perfect strangers as they paddle past. It's simultaneously liberating and laughable.

Taking time out for pooping is a necessary evil when camping away from facilities. I can't cover every tactic, but let's explore some practical approaches to poop.

First, be physically comfortable with the "third-world squat." Practice at home. Keep your feet flat, angled away from your rump. Get your backside as low to the ground as possible. Throw your upper weight forward. Drape your arms over your knees to feel it balance out. Rest your armpits or elbows on your knees. If you're not physically able to squat—practice. Squat for several minutes to stretch and strengthen your quads. You should be able to go down and back up unassisted. This position is not only the best for bowel movements but a handy low stance for around the camp kitchen or while fire-building to avoid the dirt or wet ground.

Catholes are easy to excavate in soft earth. The darker the soil, the quicker your deposit will decompose. However, the dusty ground of the alpine is difficult to dig. It's compact, tough, rocky, and lacks organic materials found under tree cover. As an alternative, I've resorted to utilizing the holes vacated by half-sunken volleyball-sized rocks. When a good-sized rock wiggles, you're onto something—there's a chance you can roll it. The deeper the cavity the better. These make-shift catholes can save you from the dig. *Slowly* replacing the rock to its original orientation achieves a few benefits. Rather than being buried in a pile, the mess is evenly spread under the rock, increasing its surface area and decomposition rate. Second, the stone acts as a natural rodent barrier.

Critters are attracted to buried poop and dig it up after you leave. I've stumbled into these dig sites several times with strewn toilet paper. It's not because the camper didn't dig or bury, but the "mini bears" undid their deed. Years ago, I validated my hypothesis while checking into a Yellowstone ranger station before heading seven miles into a remote river canyon. They recommended not only burying your business but capping it with rocks as the small mammals were being conditioned to stir it back up. Last step: toss a branch on your stash, so your buddy doesn't turn over the same stone. Letting others know your general direction keeps waste randomized.

Have your paper, wipes, hand sanitizer, and other washing methods laid out and ready before take-off. A squat is a balancing act. With arms flung forward, you'll want each toiletry within arm's reach. Although you're balancing, take time to do clean-up right. A dirty bum quickly chaffs, gets irritated, and makes for a miserable existence. Use a spritz of water and scrub if needed. You're going to wash your hands regardless afterward. Whenever practical, bring used wipes straight to the campfire as they take much longer to biodegrade, irrespective of marketing claims.

Lastly, after stirring, burying, covering, and making the site unattractive to campers and critters, don't touch your face. Get yourself cleaned up with water, soap, sand, sanitizer, and do whatever it takes to avoid contact until you're cleansed. Most backcountry eating is hand-delivered without utensils. At that moment, your hands are the biggest threat to your physical health and often the primary cause of giardia, as discussed earlier. Come back to camp with a fresh bum and fresh hands. High-fives all around! (Ok, maybe not.)

When too many days have passed or your cathole cleaning tactics aren't up to snuff, it's time to get your body a little wetter and a little more lathered.

The Coldest Bath

I equate swimming in frigid lakes and rivers for refreshment and hygiene to a good workout, choosing a healthy snack, or getting up early—I never want to do it instinctively, but I never regret each time it's done. Without fail, I think to myself, "That felt great! I should do it more often!" Then I forget the next opportunity. Such is life.

Walks through the woods are magical by themselves with the vistas and solitude, but when a few ingredients come together to make a swim happen, memories abound. The key elements are a warm sunny afternoon, an inviting swimming hole, and sticky skin covered in a couple of days of repellent, sweat, and dust.

Admittedly, I'm usually the last to take the plunge. If copious peer pressure is required to get you to jump into a cold lake, you're not the only one. I trek with friends and family who have surprisingly high tolerances to shockingly cold water. I've accepted my role as the last one in and the first one out.

There are three methods to clean that will carry you through days without a shower: the face bath, the full submerge, and the squat bath. Each has its purpose depending on need, time, weather, and fun.

The face bath is recommended daily, preferably when you're done hiking and sweating for the day, but before the sun goes down. Soap is optional but helpful. Your cotton handkerchief is the only tool needed. Stand over the water and get your face close. Splash your nostrils, ears, eyes, and hair. If you can taste the salty sweat running into the side of your mouth, you're doing it right. Wet your handkerchief as a washcloth. Wipe the back of your neck and collar. Wring it out as needed until your face is refreshed, cold, and your hair is standing on end. With the wet cloth, wipe your legs, especially between your thighs. If you neglect this step, you'll notice how leg oils tend to get sticky when together in your sleeping bag. If the sun is up, you'll be dry in minutes. Hang your handkerchief up for the night. It'll be bone-dry in the morning, ready to swab tomorrow's sweat.

The full submerge is intimidating and memorable. If there's a short cliff entry available, it can be the highlight of the week. Backcountry swims can be done barefoot, buck-naked, or with shoes and underwear, depending on groundcover and comfort level. A daring dress code only compounds the entertainment value of cold water. Skinny-dipping is liberating even if unexpected fellow hikers walk by. I've never been on the giving or receiving end of that awkward encounter, but I suppose I'd say, "It's okay. It's nothing you've never seen before."

Before your sunny swim, prepare your dry-off area. Have a down jacket ready or a cozy beanie. Bring your repellent. Find a slab of stone and pin your clothes down with smaller rocks. More than once, an unexpected maritime breeze has threatened to soak my shirt by nearly tossing it into the drink while I'm bathing. Carry a sample of biodegradable body wash that can lather your hair and pits clean—no need for shampoo, conditioner, or additional toiletries. You just need something to break up the oil layer. And no need to tote the whole bottle. A few quarter-sized dabs in a mini container will scrub you for a swim or two for a one-week trip. Nothing more than a motel offers is required.

If you're in it for a quick dip and want to minimize time spent in frigid water, start by standing ankle-deep and do a "splash bath." Lather from top to literal bottom—hair, pits, then cracks. Once you're a soapy mess and the suds are getting in your eyes, don't torture yourself with a gradual rocky wade to deeper water—a death by a thousand cuts— buck-up and plunge in over your head. Once you're back on your feet and have your breath, scrub all the soap away. Rinse by immersion. Swim as long as you can stand it. There's a healing aspect to cold water on sore muscles. You won't regret it!

Fearless Jared leaps off an inviting cliff into a high lake near 10,000 feet.

While standing on your drying slab, you'll curse each breeze and find yourself praying to the sun gods to stay that approaching cloud. Use your handkerchief to increase surface area. It won't dry you like a towel, more of a smear and air-dry method. Spread your wings and turn like a rotisserie chicken until toasty. Notice how amazing your skin feels. All the swelling, stickiness, and soreness is gone. You're a new and more civilized creature. Now grab your camera and capture the moment for the group.

The squat bath wasn't discovered until recently. And therein is a lesson all its own. Even after thousands of miles trekked, you can be learning new skills. "I'm definitely doing that next time" is a thought you want to have every trip. In this case, necessity was the mother of invention. I had enjoyed a midday swim and felt refreshed on day three. But the afternoon included a few miles of dusty trail and a toilet break that (how do I say this) didn't leave me with that "fresh feeling." I didn't want to enter my sleeping bag with dirty feet and monkey butt. The sun was going down behind a cloud wall and an evening breeze was whipping up. It was not swimming weather.

I wanted to rinse my toes in the shallows of the lake but considered how doing a third-world squat in foot-deep water would solve two problems at once. I could not only give my toes a rinse but simultaneously soak my bum and groin bidet-style. Using the running water in the shallows of a decent-sized stream is ideal for this method rather than a stagnant lake. The result was remarkable. The third-world squat bath cleanses all the grungiest parts of your body at day's end without chilling your warm core. Whether lakeside or streamside, select barefoot-friendly gravel or slabbed rock bottom to avoid adding mud between the toes. Dipping your derriere still takes your breath away but doesn't require perfect weather to dry the entire body like after a swim. It has the benefits of the full submerge without the shell shock. Five stars—will do again!

Whatever your skin-scrub strategy, savor your cool, dry, goose-bumped skin while you can. It won't be long until you'll need to reapply insect repellent. Your breath and warm flesh will soon attract the buzzing bane of the animal kingdom.

Biting Back at Bugs

If I could wave a magic wand and instantly change anything about the American backcountry, mosquitos would be immediately extinct. I reckon I'm not alone in this fantasy. I'm sure an environmental scientist could explain their crucial ecological purpose, but I'm unwilling to listen. Instead, I figure that all good things in life, like primitive public land loaded with impressive peaks and wild rivers, have costs. Every rose has its thorn. The price tag for being in big beautiful mountains is biting insects.

There is hope. Each week you spend living among them, you'll find yourself becoming more tolerant, less bothered, and savvier about avoidance. The point will come when you get bit; you shrug your shoulders and move on. While certainly not immune, you'll see the irritants through a lens of acquired resilience. You'll be reminded of this when you're with someone new to living among mosquitos. While all use spray and take practical precautions, novice trekkers will regularly complain, showcasing lower tolerance. It's not a point of pride but an indicator that you can look forward to after additional years of increased resilience. Don't let the persistent pests govern your happiness. Push through as biting bugs, like sore muscles and steep trails, are part of the overall experience.

Not pictured: droves of mosquitos that made enjoying this vista short-lived.

Luckily mosquitos have a fleeting life expectancy. It's a graph that rises and drops sharply. Knowing the pattern can help you avoid the peaks and enjoy the tranquil times. They hatch with the snowmelt starting in the arid southern states and pop up last near Canada. They hatch from south to north with the warming season, and from low to high in elevation. Swarms peak mid-summer, and for most states, by mid-August, their numbers are markedly diminished, making more pleasurable conditions. By Labor Day weekend, biting bugs are noticeably gone.

The last few summers I've enjoyed weeklong treks during the latter half of August where I could count the number of mosquitos in single digits. I never needed sticky spray all week. However, the few times I popped above 11,000 feet between basins, they were thriving. The hatch follows the thaw upward. High ridges are the last to grow grass and thereby the latest to host the pests. Conversely, in late June and early July, you'll find them below the timberline hatching heavily in the forest canopy, but once you get above 10,500 feet, the hatch is still weeks away as you camp among stronghold snow patches.

DEET-based products are the industry standard for repellent. The lighter-caliber sprays (12-20%) are great for skin and kids but lack the firepower when thick swarms descend in the peak of mosquito season. There are backcountry versions (25-40%) marketed for the dense swarms but use with caution on your face. 100% DEET is available but not recommended for skin and corrosive to plastics and fishing line.

After ruining polarized sunglasses by touching the frames after applying DEET-based repellent and worrying about compromising fishing line integrity and clothing finishes, I no longer used the toxic solution. There are a few competitive alternatives like picaridin and permethrin to test. These more modern solutions have equivalent repellent strengths without the chemical stench and drawbacks. Some brands genuinely smell pleasant to apply. Testing has shown them at least as strong against swarms as everything requires occasional re-application.

Don't buy aerosols. You get more product for your dollars with pumps and lotions. And even with that spray bottle, don't spray your face. No one's any good at aiming those tiny spray nozzles. You'll waste less into thin air by merely spraying your palms generously first, then applying like liquid lotion. This sensible method saves you from tasting it, wasting it, or burning your eyeballs during application. Since it's a liquid, it's a bit heavy for the ounce-counter, but liquid gold regardless. A three-ounce pump bottle of 20% picaridin is about the perfect amount for a week, even in thick swarms. I've come close, but never needed a second bottle even when reapplying daily.

The best ingredient to your biting bug repellent plan isn't a chemical spray or what week you hike, but clothing. Fabric is not only the best sunblock but also the best mosquito repellent, though all clothing isn't impenetrable. The mosquitos' needle-like proboscis easily pierces some thinner breathable fabrics. Materials like fleece, nylon, and other synthetic blends have a thick or tight enough weave to protect your skin, but loosely woven wool socks or polyester hiking shirts can be speared.

How do you know? Hold it up to a light.

If light easily permeates, cover it with spray or expect a sting. That three-ounce bottle works for me because on a given day, I'm only reapplying repellent to a few spots: the backs of hands, socks near ankles, shirts near triceps and shoulders, exposed ears and neck—that's it. The rest is covered. I rarely hike in shorts or short-sleeve shirts for a few reasons to be reviewed.

You have two choices out there: ideal weather or no mosquitoes. You can choose only one—never both. If you're getting bit, congratulations, you're likely currently enjoying mild temperatures near room temperature with little-to-no wind. Mosquitos not only have pathetic lifespans but are embarrassingly sensitive to extremes in direct sunlight, heat, cold, or wind. If you're having any of these, enjoy the break from bugs. However, deer flies, horse flies, and black flies, although not as common, seem to revel in warmer temps. Their bites burn unnoticed at first, increasing in pain until nearly unbearable. Fortunately, they don't arrive in swarms and are dispatched one by one. Sprays work, but a quick karate chop or a wingman watching your six works better.

My teenage son was hiking in front of me on a bluebird day above the timberline. A steady breeze came head-on keeping us from feeling the heat as we followed the trail.

Looking down at my shadow, I saw its shadow. A lurking horsefly enjoyed our scent and stayed out of sight in the windbreak we created for it. Experience has taught me to watch my shadow for these hovering bugs as they try to land unnoticed. It set down harmlessly on the top of my son's backpack lid, offering a convenient attack angle for my right-handed kill shot. Even with warning, the impact startled my son. The fly dropped dead on the trail, only to be replaced by another micro drone a minute later. Once again, it landed on his pack, and "whack" another one was down. As we walked along the cirque, it was like I've never seen it elsewhere. Nevermore than one at a time, they came to be killed.

The death toll was seven.

He doesn't remember much else from that 9-mile day except "Remember that lake with the horse flies?"

CHAPTER 8
NUTRITIONAL NEEDS

I enjoy delicious food. Who doesn't? The flavors, caloric density, and nutrition available in the modern world are unmatched.

Unfortunately, this vast variety requires refrigeration, cooking systems, and kitchen implements impossible to expect in the wild. Instead, backpackers go into survival mode when finding their daily fare. We look for proven basics and satisfying staples.

Approaching what to eat while in the backcountry requires some semblance of strategy and planning. It doesn't demand perfection, but certainly something more than I attempted in my early miles when I would order fast food on approach to the trailhead, request them without soggy condiments, then stuff them in my 70-liter backpack, hoping they'd be safe to eat several hours later for dinner. I've evolved over the decades from haphazard leftovers, to predictable packaged meals, to a diet based on whole foods.

Credit where credit's due, I gleaned much of my backcountry mentorship from studying the decades of experiences shared in Rich Osthoff's book, *Fly-Fishing the Rocky Mountain Backcountry.* I can't recommend this book enough. His eloquent stories inspire adventure for any angler interested in trekking beyond well-trodden streamside trails. And when it comes to eating, his approach to a no-cook menu breaks the paradigm of stoves, freeze-dried meals, and kitchenware. I was stuck in the rut of boiling water each evening before reading his recommendations.

It doesn't take a book to learn how to hydrate bagged beef stroganoff. Nor will this book impress with fancy recipes. Prepare to be disappointed if you're looking for creative ideas to enhance your menu. You'll have to seek them elsewhere. Outdoor magazines and online articles are filled with beautifully photographed and "Insta-worthy" dishes portrayed in the foreground of stunning wilderness backdrops. Like the four-bean fiesta bowl or Thai curry chicken pasta, these trendy recipes look and sound delicious, but I'm not out there to cook or combine ingredients. I came to play.

Everyone needs to approach backpacking with their purpose. The pragmatic in me has a simple mission: push myself into remote areas to explore, hike, and fish in otherwise untouched wilderness. The sensible approach to eating along the way is unromantic, a mere means to health and strength to achieve said mission. Eating is not an event unto itself.

In the wilderness, new culinary criteria emerge. Menus are no longer led by flavor and craving, as may be the case at home. Taste isn't tossed aside but instead settles for a secondary measure. Pragmatics judge on-the-go snacks and sit-down meals by realism. They need minimal preparation and a short ingredients list. Assembly should be uncomplicated, foolproof, and preferably nonexistent. Real-world food for trekking should be weighted on basic characteristics like packability, nutritional density, weight, durability, ease of clean-up, and weather resilience. Items are elevated in value as they check as many of these boxes as possible.

Nutrient density should top the list. What is this food providing me? As this sport is an athletic endurance experience, mind your balance of protein grams, complex and simple carbohydrates, fiber, and other essential nutrients. The more healthful nutrition you consume, the stronger you'll feel. Avoid leaning on the empty calories found in sugar-rich snacks and shelf-stable junk foods. Sugary or salty snacks have their place but are best paired with something power packed. Staying on top of your protein consumption will prevent next-day muscle fatigue. Balancing slow- and fast-burning carbs will help stave off your legs from red-lining and can generate that second wind.

Protein should be found in every meal and nearly every snack. The average sedentary woman or man needs 45 to 55 grams per day, respectively. With the increased activity involved in backpacking, those needs are increased by 50% or more, depending on your itinerary. Once you've assembled your menu, do some quick math to ensure you're giving your body what it needs in the protein department.

Packability is a top-tier cuisine criterion. Flat foods are rated highest, like apricot fruit leather, spinach wraps, or Spam sleeves. They require minimal real estate. Every cubic inch is precious when seeking to minimize your pack's mass. Once inside a snack-sized sandwich baggie, gently flattening curvy tortilla chips may ruin their look, but they are just as tasty when half the size and twice as packable. For variety, rotate wheat or cheesy crackers which also fit the bill as highly packable, square-and-salty carb snacks tucked in a baggie. Avoid strong-flavored varieties of chips and crackers. Flavor-coated crunchy snacks are great along the trail but don't offer the same versatility as their mild counterparts to be added to wraps or crushed into hot meals for extra crunch without overtaking the meal's taste.

Dried seaweed is a pleasing side for any dinner. Although oily and salty, they help me feel like I'm eating some sort of vegetable. Individual servings come in a boxy, protective, plastic tray but are easily transferred flat into a snack-sized baggie. Like chips and crackers, they taste the same smashed but offer increased space savings. Don't be afraid to repackage foods but use caution. Once factory seals are broken, the clock starts ticking on moisture and mold.

Pre-cooked shelf-stable bacon is a must-carry. Some grocery stores camouflage it in the cold section with other bacon that requires refrigeration. Others will store it on a shelf nearby. Ditch the cardboard package and slide the vacuum-sealed bag into your menu for midweek. Once you crack it open, it's a full, one-night commitment. It can't go back in your bag. Have a bacon celebration and enjoy all 12 slices with the group or make it that night's protein. They taste great cold, but if you're bored or want to get fancy, try searing them over a fire for some sizzle.

One downside to prepackaged foods is their tendency to inflate when packaged at lower altitudes, then hiked over summits. The air pressure around you lessens as you ascend, yielding the internal pressure to expand from where they were packaged. You may find a factory-sealed bar or bag nearly ready to explode when opened above 11,000 feet. And it's not just today's snack. Each sealed item in the following day's rations is inflating your pack.

The solution is simple. Before stuffing snacks with excess air into your supplies, pierce a tiny hole in the corner with a safety pin. Slowly squeeze out the excess air. Compression not only reduces their initial packing size but allows them to "breathe" with dramatic changes in altitude. The hack works for small packages of cookies and large jerky bags, especially when pierced above a resealable top. Don't carry air. If your cookies or snacks get a little smashed, so what!

Caution: don't divvy-up commercial beef jerky into individual baggies for each day. Keep it in the original pouch or suffer everything tasting like jerky after a few days. I learned this the hard way, enduring jerky-flavored everything.

Assign yourself one resealable gallon bag per day. Use a marker to dedicate it to a day or number. I like using numbers to help me forget what day of the week it is—a small symbolic way to get lost from the regular world when wandering in the wild.

What day is it? Day 5.

No. What *day* of the week? It doesn't matter.

What am I doing today? Not going to work, that's for sure. I'll probably hike, fish, and sleep, in that order.

Fill your daily bags with dinner first and breakfast last— first in, last out. Except for a few exceptions, like a weeklong resealable feedbag of dried apples or jerky, this gallon bag is your day's rations. Once it's stuffed and ready to seal shut, leave a small gap to suck out any stubborn last bits of air like a human vacuum sealer. You'll be surprised how funny you look and how much it reduces the bulk. Remember, unless you're dropping altitude into the red gravel switchbacks of the Grand Canyon, it's going to inflate with elevation. Place today's bag atop your pack to help you stay organized and avoid rummaging for snacks along the trail. Having today's bag handy increases trail speed and steadies your caloric intake.

Ration organization is completed by taking each vacuum-sealed gallon bag and stacking them last-to-first in a lightweight food bag. There are a few options here. At a minimum, a high-stretch grocery sack works, but only from stores that use thicker plastics. I've done entire weeks with quality Target bags doubled-up. One better, a thin reusable fabric grocery sack is my latest preference. Some use nylon stuff sacks from a sleeping bag (obviously not from the bag you're toting). The bulkiest and most durable solution is a hard-sided bear canister. Regardless of your bag choice, it needs to endure being tied to a rope and raised into trees to avoid attracting omnivores. And don't leave tops too loose while hung. Nightly rainstorms will fill the bottom. My food bag tops the interior of my pack to minimize a week of bumps and bruises.

Even if you're not in a bear management area, hang your food. Every critter is glad you made it. Like a dog in a kitchen, birds and mammals patiently await your unmonitored food or neglected crumbs. I've been both impressed and perturbed witnessing the crafty antics of the brave gray jay. This winged camp marauder is unabashed along with every chipmunk and ground squirrel around. Some "mini bears" are downright naughty.

After a day of fly-fishing deep in the belly of Colorado's Black Canyon of the Gunnison, our group returned to our sandy campsite for dinner. There were socks and sacks strewn between our three dome tents. Wrappers and remnants littered the ground. There had been an invasion. Upon inspection of the damage, the nylon door to my solo tent had been chewed clean through. I had errantly left a day's worth of food in my tent, confident there were no bears in the hot canyon. With my door zipped shut, the local family of golden-mantled ground squirrels chiseled a new opening. We had been hit by a Category-4 squirrel storm afterward dubbed "Hurricane Squirrelina." Duct tape patched the hole. My favorite tent was irreparable. My buddies were generous enough to share their portions to get me through another day. The round rainbow trout were worth it. Lesson learned: hang your food.

The caution isn't just for food bags. Assume everything you leave out for the night or during a day hike will be inspected — or tasted. Last summer, I learned this on the final morning of a six-day loop through the Wind River mountains. I casually left out my favorite collapsible blue silicon cup. Confident I had scrubbed any spaghetti sauce out of it from dinner; I left it out to drip dry all night. The next morning, hot oatmeal leaked through it to my hands. I suspected I had worn out the hinges with overuse or scratched it. Upon further inspection, several edges of the silicon had identifiable double incisor bite marks from a field mouse gnawing off every last flavor remnant while I slept feet away. Time for a new cup and a renewed commitment to clean up the kitchen completely.

Durability and **weather resistance** are critical traits. Everything you bring needs to be tough enough to withstand daily bundling, compression, rain, rummaging, and drops. Nothing can be at risk of leakage. If something is bruised or broken, it still needs to be edible.

Likewise, your food needs to withstand heat. Chilly weather doesn't damage food. In fact, colder temps preserve fresh food. But when miles are marched under a scorching summer sun, chocolate snacks melt into a mess. I've entirely stopped carrying my favorite chocolate items. They're decent for a few days, but after being hung in a tree for an exploration day or suffocated under hot pack fabric for another, they're no fun. String cheese is better kept in cool weather but holds up surprisingly well over a week. Night temps cool it daily. Even when eaten warm, they get a little oily but still taste great, offering useful protein and salty flavor.

Bread is relatively lightweight and loaded with complex carbohydrates and other nutrients but is bulky and easily smashed. Use whole-wheat wraps, flatbreads, and soft tortillas as they store flat, are foldable, and durable. These gluten staples are prone to mold. It doesn't happen often, but in the case of mold, pick off the edges or feed the curious gray jay on extended trips. By then, you should be ready to start a new sealed package anyway.

Weight has been the primary characteristic touted by the popular freeze-dried meal industry. A warm entrée for two is packaged in just four to five ounces. The practicality of that so-called serving size is debatable. Size correlates with how much water is added to make the meal—two cups counts as two servings. Hungry adults will undoubtedly need more than a cup of soupy pasta or rice to be satisfied after a hiking day. Treat two servings as what would equate to a plate-full of food.

Serving arguments aside, the alleged weight savings contradiction is similarly glaring. A weighty stove system is required to boil the two cups of water needed to make those lightweight ingredients into warm entrées. The pot, fuel canister, stove, and tools can exceed a pound, add to pack bulk, and come with mechanical failure risks.

Rich Osthoff challenged this paradigm in his book by abandoning the need for stoves and instead carrying slightly heavier ready-to-eat meat. As he outlines, hot breakfast and lunches at home are rare, so taking stove gear for one hot meal a day is inefficient. His no-cook menu suggestions flip the freeze-dried script.

Like his experience, I have found the overall weight savings to be modest, but I saw a marked increase in nutritional value, taste, ease of preparation, reduced pack bulk, clutter, and cost.

Freeze-dried meals are pricey. A six-ounce tear pouch of tuna weights almost the same but comes with half the mass, a quarter the price, twice the protein, and fresh-meat satisfaction. You can find tear pouches with tuna, salmon, chicken, and bacon in most grocery stores. Eating them straight from the bag can get dull and dry. With a long spork, stir in gas station mayonnaise, mustard, relish, salt, and pepper. Roll onto a whole-wheat flatbread or spinach wrap. Layer in ripped string cheese, bacon strips, crumbled chips, or all three when you're feeling fancy and ready to go deluxe. Biting into this backcountry wrap never gets old as the protein and chips change every night. It's fresh, meaty, chewy, crunchy, saucy, and satiating. It's always filling and has little clean-up. One six-ounce meat pouch makes two good-sized wraps. Chunk light or chunk white tuna stirs easier than whole albacore.

That's the extent of the recipes you'll find here. The remainder of my no-cook menu is as follows.

Breakfast is overnight-soaked oatmeal with honey and nut packets from Starbucks. Soft-dried apple rings, banana chips, or mango slices round out morning snacks. Starting the day chewing minty gum after breakfast makes me feel downright civilized.

Lunch starts early along the trail and is a walking lunch — rarely a sit-down meal. Before leaving breakfast, I fill my cargo pockets with lunch like a squirrel stuffing its cheeks. Okay, maybe not to that extent.

Later along the trail, I reach in and pull out whatever I assigned myself. Walking-lunch staples include a peanut butter squeeze pouch, a quality protein bar (changing the flavor daily), and fruit leather. A baggie of salted almonds mixed with dried blueberries is a hard-to-beat sweet-and-salty mix. If not, classic trail mix works, but beware melting the chocolate M&Ms. Beef jerky is the protein staple. I chew it randomly throughout the day. Select mild flavors as the strong stuff gets old after a few days.

Dinner is based on the tear-pouch wrap, as mentioned. The stirring and rolling can all happen quickly in my lap or on a clean flat slab of natural granite countertop as a table to keep out the grit. Watch that first bite, though. If rolled improperly, all of your precious juices and condiments will leak out the back. Sides are crumbled corn chips, crackers, string cheese, repackaged dried seaweed, and a small package of mini cookies for the inevitable sweet tooth.

If it's late in the journey and I'm ready for some salty and fatty meat, I'll slide a slot or two of Spam into my gullet. It's not the highest-grade meat, but it's incredibly durable and satiating. Sprinkling Spam with fast food pepper packets takes it up a notch. Skip the salt—it's baked in.

If in a group and the weight of fuel, stove, and kitchenware can be shared, I enjoy freeze-dried pasta meals as well as belly-warming instant potatoes.

Wrapping Up

This real-world wrap routine makes up for what it lacks in daily variety with dependability, durability, function, and speed. It is stormproof and sensible enough to snarf down under the dry side of a lodgepole pine during a downpour.

Be mindful that dinner is the most likely to be challenged with a late-blooming afternoon thunderstorm.

You'll find the only variation day to day may be the flavor of the protein bar, the kind of chips, or the type of meat in your wrap. Otherwise, this menu is built for the culinary creature of habit whose priorities are enjoying every precious day off seeking adventure, not soaking pasta.

On average, the no-cook menu works out to be about a pound per day, sometimes a bit more. A week's rations average about nine pounds. After six or seven days without hot food, save only the occasional fish, you'll understandably be craving a piping-hot cheeseburger upon exit. But the same cravings come after a week of hot freeze-dried food. For example, I've never blown past a burger joint while driving home, thinking, "I'm good. I had two whole cups of runny re-hydrated lasagna last night."

Don't validate the concern that not consuming hot food somehow depletes you in that short of time. On the contrary, I argue that the fresh proteins and flatbreads found in a meaty no-cook menu leave me stronger overall. The only difference is that I'm not soon stopping at Subway for a footlong tuna salad sandwich.

Living Off the Land

Even if you are angling daily, regularly eating off the land by flame-broiling trout is impractical for the same reasons discussed with campfire maintenance. Besides, cleaning and cooking fish generates attractive scents for critters great and small. I'd rather exist unbothered by rodents and without looking over my shoulder for a bruin.

On average, a weeklong trip may find occasion for one fresh-cooked meal of trout. And it's usually on a layover day in an area ripe with a high concentration of decent-sized fish.

Trout living in alpine lakes dwell in a delicate balance of food supply and population density—quantity and quality. Rare exceptions aside, high-altitude lakes support fish in two categories: high populations of smaller-sized trout or sparsely populated lakes with larger or trophy-class trout. Avoid eating from the latter. Better to eat two smaller fish than one brute to avoid throwing off nature's balance.

When you cook one, be prepared with a folded rectangle of heavy-duty foil rather than the regular more puncture-prone variety. If you ever find real butter in individual serving packs, grab them. KFC is one of the only places I've located margarine in small squeeze packets. Experience has taught me that it's tough to over-bake trout. Like marinating mushrooms, they get better with time. Medium-rare fish meat isn't dangerous to eat, and certainly moister, but you'll find that when left on the fire longer, the flesh gets flakier, the skin gets crispier, and the burnt edges offer that gristly flavor your body craves.

One Note on Number Two

Backpacking foods tend to be high in plant-based fiber. These meals and snacks include oatmeal, dried fruits, berries, whole wheat, nuts, and seeds. Fiber is an essential nutrient but can soften stools quickly. No one enjoys irritable bowels, especially without facilities. It's not a pleasant topic but needs to be addressed.

If you manage to find yourself in this situation after day two and beyond, you don't have giardia; your system is accustomed to eating far less fiber. Find relief in small doses of a daily anti-diarrheal like Imodium or chewable Pepto. Ideally, it balances the fiber overload. Frankly, I'm thankful when it does a bit more than that by shutting my system down for the rest of the day. I don't mind taking a day off from a churning gut.

Neither digestive extreme is recommendable, but if I had to choose, erring on the side of seldom and solid is far more comfortable in the backcountry than runny and regular. As it has averted mountain misery more than once, this medicine has earned a top spot as one of two essential remedies in my kit. It's second only to before-bed ibuprofen. I need neither at home but lean on both in the wilderness to recover before sunrise.

CHAPTER 9
COMMUNICATION & SAFETY

The perfect hiking partner is an extraordinary treasure, a rare gem. Two different individuals have to align varied physical abilities, agree on objectives, navigate conflicting work schedules, and settle on shared leadership roles. Each person included beyond two increases friendships and camaraderie but adds calendar variables, preparation risks, and potential threes-a-crowd committee politics.

There's something magnetic about a backpacking expedition. Each member is drawn to inviting a child, a coworker, or a friend. It's socially awkward to share your excitement for an upcoming adventure without feeling obliged to say, "You should come!"

Suddenly, groups of four turn to six, then six into eight at the last minute. Aligning the stars to create a group vacation is difficulty multiplied but can have an immense payout if pulled off successfully.

I've trekked a third of my distances solo, a third with one buddy, and the remainder in a group, the largest being a 15-

person youth group. Most were groups of five or six family members and close friends. Only once have I met a friend-of-a-friend for the first time at the trailhead.

The benefits of groups include deepened memories between friends and family. A lasting bond of survival is cemented among those who have subsisted on so little for days on end. Shared struggles, inside jokes, laughter, and physical successes permanently seal stories together. When one member's legs aren't feeling strong, their equipment can be spread out to alleviate fatigue. One pair can gather bottles to filter water for the group while others scavenge for dry firewood. Food variety is relished as extra portions are distributed. A few anglers on a lakeshore can spot more cruisers and test twice the fly patterns to see what's working.

Groups also have risks that balance their benefits. The number one risk to a prosperous group trek isn't the weakest among them, it's the enthusiastic organizer who overestimates individual capabilities and places the least experienced in harm's way. Group leaders are generally the most experienced, the most in-shape, and the most likely to cajole a few beyond their ability. Guard yourself against becoming this optimistically inconsiderate frontrunner. Likewise, protect yourself from being the least experienced hiker on a lung-pumping death march.

The hypothesis that "there is safety in numbers" does not apply to backpacking, even as dangerous as solo backpacking sounds. The larger the group, the statistically more likely a physical injury will occur, not only because of sheer numbers, but the increased probability that the group's experience is diametrical. The larger the group, the more likely the novice among them will find themselves scrambling to pace with the proficient. This conditioning contrast creates an environment for injury. Conversely, if everyone's new to the sport, their natural pace will be more approachable for all invited—likewise for a cluster of pros wanting to swiftly hammer out mileage. There is safety in numbers, so long as the numbers are equally experienced and similar in speed.

Find balance in smaller groups. Draw a safe circle of those you trust to lead or those you can count on to follow. Groups conquer common preparation pitfalls with equipment shakedown nights, short out-and-back campouts, and friendly physical conditioning challenges. Additionally, there is leave-no-trace wisdom in little clusters of campers as they minimize impact and move near-undetected through the wilderness.

Two-person teams are hard to top. A three-pack is good company. Foursomes form handy divisions when buddy systems are needed for two-man tents or dual-serving shared meals. There is no magic number, but each addition as the group grows should add increased consideration and precaution for potential disparities in physical conditioning, preparation, experience, expectations, and mental fortitude.

In larger companies of six to a dozen, there will inevitably be those who sprint out of the gate and want to trailblaze with reckless abandon—literally abandoning, then waiting repeatedly. They may be the most in shape, have the longest gate, or have an unchecked sense of competitiveness. Every group has one. On the other end of the dusty pack train, there will be the gatherer who ensures none are left behind and, although they may have the strength to be the lead dog, choose to carefully close-up shop behind the group, gathering granola bar wrapper corners fallen from pockets and nursing the needy. In groups this size, a good rule is to ask the adrenaline alpha to freeze at every fork. Any sign, split, ford, or major landmark gets a brake check, lest a critical course change is missed, and the group is divided unendingly. A better rule is to have them slow down if they can't see or hear the last hiker.

Twice on the same few miles of a popular trail I've declared the stop-at-every-fork rule, and twice it has cost hours wasted on day one, wondering which trail the pedal-to-the-metal hikers selected. Eventually, they doubled back to find the back half of the group. Both times, the lecture was rehearsed.

Good: stop at each fork.

Better: stay in sight of the last.

Best: be patient and stay together.

Another group-savvy system is to travel in leap-frog fashion, rather than caterpillar style. When those in front stop to fumble with shoelaces or hydration hoses, mid-group hikers should feel free to keep marching. When the who's-in-front-of-who order is enforced and all stop, it creates caterpillar-like concussions of stop-and-go traffic as the group inchworms down the trail for hours. Plan on one mile an hour at best when inch-worming. Leapfrogging allows everyone to stop as needed without obligating others to stay in order. It shortens excessive breaks and allows friends who may be feeling their second wind to open up their stride.

Interactions along the trail shouldn't be all oriented around safety and order. One of the biggest rewards to group treks is how it lends itself to relationship building. It's been in the confidentiality of wilderness that I've felt the most safety in opening up with hiking companions. Shared experiences deepen dialogues as you move miles. Strengthen your relationships with honest expressions, shared hopes and fears, through old-fashioned, face-to-face verbal communication.

Backpacking Solo

When you're ready to test your mental mettle, experience heavenly and haunting solitude, and feel your safety skills are up for it, try a solo trek.

A few Julys ago, I accomplished a personal record—a seven-day solo expedition. A trek of this length may be blasé for other solo backpackers, but it meant a great deal to me. I had spent several previous summers testing smaller jaunts, working up to three- and four-day solo adventures. The majority of this 65-mile route was off-trail. And somehow, I managed to sign myself up for 1,000-foot hurdles each day as I popped from one rugged drainage to the next. It was not just the lengthiest solo experience I had ever had, but the most physically challenging. It's an unsettling and liberating feeling going days without seeing anyone. The best part of routes with passes is sitting atop each wind-swept saddle, peering down over where you've wandered the day prior.

One benefit and risk of creating only one set of footsteps is wildlife encounters. While strolling through a thick forest that reeked of elk musk, I carelessly popped into a meadow where a dozen cow elk were drinking. I had the wind in my favor and stood frozen, savoring every second undetected. Never had I stumbled so close to elk, known for their radar senses. Once the gaze of the matriarch pinged me, the earth shook as they rumbled into the cover of timber. The encounter would not have occurred in a chatty group of two or three buddies stomping through the brush.

However, the solo backpacker must be vigilant in bear country to make their presence no surprise. That herd of elk could have just as easily been a grizzly interrupted while feasting on an elk carcass. Startling a feeding bruin is second only to the danger of marching near her cubs. Clapping, whistling, and talking all work well to announce your approach. I enjoy singing to my heart's content, often the same verse repetitively, with the same no-one's-watching vigor found in the safety of a commuting car. When bushwhacking through timber where visibility makes you nervous, carry a baseball bat-sized stick and swing away at fallen branches, sending the crack echoing forward.

Making noise helps you avoid unwanted encounters. Chatter and laughter among small groups lift spirits and keeps everyone safer, but more often than not, I long for silence. I speak for the millions who work in social professions and find themselves initiating—or enduring—conversations much of each workday. The allure of silence starts early in the solitary drive to the trailhead. Hours pass as the mind is soothed by the highway's rhythmic hum, sans playlist and news radio.

Silence also leads to loneliness—an unadmitted deterrent for the solo-trekking curious. The abrupt absence of conversation, constant messaging, social media, and news cycles can be jarring. Existing alone with your thoughts, without Wi-Fi connectivity nor human connection, takes practice.

Being alone and suffering loneliness are two very different experiences. It's possible to be alone without feeling lonely. Both sensations can surface on a solo journey but classifying emotions into rational, irrational, selfish, and unselfish compartments prolongs mental health and enjoyment. As you evolve negative thoughts from an inward focus to an outward observance of surroundings and gratitude for the present, self-centered loneliness gives way to confidence while existing—and thriving—alone.

Once mental hurdles are hushed and physical safety is trained, the pragmatic benefits of solo time start to shine. What draws me back is the ease of preparation and the straightforward execution. It borders on selfishness, but it's a challenge to outdo the convenience of owning your schedule—you pick the days, the pace, the route, the agenda, the naps, the mealtimes, and the menu. There are no committee meetings to deliberate the course. Politics never arise. The lake and the trail are yours, and most importantly, the memories are private and sacred.

Scanning an unnamed lake rumored to host nice cutthroat trout.

To increase solo safety, satellite-powered beacons are advancing annually in their capability and portability. Each has a send-a-helicopter button, and some can text. However, only needing one during one week per year hardly warrants the pricey monthly subscription on top of the expensive device. A practical compromise is renting them by the week.

I save myself the subscription and enjoy the latest model with rentals. They aren't mandatory but can save lives.

At the very least, I leave my longsuffering wife with a break-glass-in-case-of-emergency envelope tucked on my nightstand. She knows to open it if she hasn't heard from me by a specific evening. It spells out contact information for county search and rescue and outlines my route, specific lake names, anticipated camping locations, clothing colors, trailheads, and a vehicle description. Fortunately, she's never needed it.

Nowadays, I've sparsely been out in the wild a week without bumping into a spotty cell signal midway to touch base.

Phoning Home

More cell towers are being erected along valley floors to compete for countrywide coverage each year. These new wireless utilities are increasing wilderness safety as they send sparse-but-functional signals deep into backcountry peaks. Carrying a cell phone should never be a safety plan as service cannot be guaranteed. However, using a topo map and aligning which canyons will have clear views of ranchland valleys below can predict signals at shocking altitudes. When strength is weak, a text message may still make it through.

If a loved one would be relieved to know you're still alive—and hopefully you're blessed enough to have someone in your life who cares—occasionally check for strong signals as you ascend ridges above the timberline. The higher you climb, the higher your chances of catching a line-of-sight signal. I've even enjoyed seamless video calls to family while hiding from whipping winds on 12,000-foot peaks. Don't forget to switch back to airplane mode when it's back to business. Phone antennas left searching for signals cause quick battery drain.

Emergency Preparedness

Each week before a trek, especially if solo, concerned coworkers and relatives ask the same questions.

"What if you get eaten by a bear?"

"What if you break your ankle and there's no one around?"

While one of those worries is statistically more plausible than the other, they both pale in comparison to the likelihood of everyday risks overlooked by the masses. Millions participate in far riskier travel without a second thought nor interrogation. Few people question these daily dangers as their occurrence isn't as sensational nor newsworthy as a bear attack or injured hiker.

The pragmatic backpacker retorts these objections remembering the real-world danger is in the 70 mile-per-hour drive to the trailhead on an unfamiliar country highway abounding in distracted drivers and darting deer. This multi-hour race is statistically more likely to injure—or heaven-forbid, kill—a backpacker than the numerous hiking days to follow. Yet people do it every hour of every day without worry. We've grown numb to common car accidents.

Keeping things in perspective doesn't justify reckless regard for personal welfare along the trail nor abandoning reasonable safety precautions. Nor should comparisons be used as a weapon to win an argument. Instead, it should settle the mind and keep cautions in the proper category— probable, possible, unlikely, or one-in-a-million. Think forgotten item, hitting a deer, wrenching an ankle, struck by lightning, in that sorted-by-likelihood order. Guard yourself accordingly and not by sensationalism.

Good fortune is not an emergency preparedness plan. Although it has followed me most of these decades, providence may be less luck and more systematic preparedness.

The more prepared the practitioners, the less they will encounter unforeseen circumstances. Staying vigilant is required, regardless of tenure, no matter the high-risk adventure. Let your guard down, and the mountain will deliver unseasonal weather, high water, fall hazards, disorientation, infestation, infection, indigestion, injury, and an endless list of other emergencies. I've endured trips with the entire list, but their presence becomes predictable with practice.

The Shoulder Boulder

When Aaron's leg rocketed deep into an unseen snowfield cavern, his pack weight crammed his shoulder into a granite boulder. As I reached him, it was apparent he would need a hand to lift himself from the slushy posthole created in the sloped snow. He tried to grasp my outstretched hand, but his upper arm didn't respond. It hung limp, lifeless, and dislocated.

It was day two of what was supposed to be a weeklong excursion to a remote drainage. Yet here we were, 15 miles from the nearest vehicle at 11,000 feet, and faced with trying to tote a big pack with a dislocated shoulder.

My mind raced to remember the maneuver to reset shoulder sockets back into place. I was sure I learned it years prior on a page in a first-aid handout.

Was it elbow-out, thumb-in, or the opposite?

Was I confusing it with Nursemaid's Elbow?

Each failed attempt stung him with pain and could potentially be making it worse. With each minute that passed, internal swelling would slowly preclude the mobility needed to reset it.

Shock started to shake his nerves as his fight-or-flight response kicked in. It didn't help that his snow-soaked shirt cooled his core in the morning breeze. Fear hovered that we may be stuck here until we get help. We weighed options to divide his pack between the other two hikers. The week's plan was abandoned, a heartbreak to our hopes and calendar count-down.

After several painful failed attempts and copious out-loud prayers, we made one last abrupt adjustment to reset the bone. He stuck out his elbow, and we wrenched his wrist skyward. The dull sound of the joint popping back into place was unsettling but medicinal music to our ears.

A few pain pills and a dry clothing layer lifted spirits. We rerouted to camp nearby and explored local lakes with lesser mileage. Each day his shoulder felt stronger. When it was clear all would be okay, it was time for hindsight reflection. We recognized the injury as generally avoidable. Edges of snowfields are the least stable, have caverns, and require trepidatious steps, not full-force strides. Aaron recalled how he was stomp-marching to make it safely across the snowy slab but didn't ease up his tread when approaching the cavernous edge.

Once home, we looked up the proper maneuver—help the injured try to touch their upper spine. We were close.

Encounters like these send countless packing out early and scare others from entering. Conversely, the triumph over danger draws the adventurous further into remote regions.

Emergency preparedness is far more mental than physical. It's a wise attitude more than a supply kit. It's in small movements throughout an activity, not an avoidance of the adventure altogether.

I am influenced by a few deductions upon reflection of what drives me toward high-risk adventures: 1) if it doesn't make me a little nervous, I lose interest, and 2) if it doesn't make me a little nervous, I let my guard down.

Ironically, I feel safer when anxiously respecting wild surroundings. When casual or careless decisions override being careful or cautious, adverse outcomes arrive. Respect affects everything from regard for ankle-spraining steps to the dismissal of hanging smellables. May your journeys be prolonged as you find good fortune from practical preparedness.

CHAPTER 10
GEAR SELECTION

Finding the right piece of gear is incredibly satisfying. The process may include the thrill of the hunt, researching options, a chase for a bargain, a bit of "retail therapy," or the emotional rush felt when finally purchasing a piece of gear that comes with a promise of use on some future adventure. New equipment offers an exciting benefit or utility not possessed previously—it's lighter, more durable, or a better fit. Each piece of gear or apparel is a tool at its core. It may save time or trouble, like a new shoe offering updated support or traction.

About a decade ago, I purchased my first high-end feather-light down jacket. Each evening, I would look forward to sliding my long arms into it and zipping it up to my chin. The instant warmth and confidence this one apparel item offered was enamoring. A running gag began by repeating the same proclamation of affection to my hiking partners each night, "Have I told you guys how much I like this jacket?"

Emotions of acquisition aside, there's a caution to gear selection. Countless hikers end up on the slippery slope of excessive expense and needless consumer clutter. Guard yourself against both sins. You don't have to stimulate the economy single-handedly, nor do you need everything each brand tries to market. Quite the opposite is true. You're selectively searching for and carrying only a few dozen items *at most*.

Take a long-term attitude into each investment. Look for the potential of extended use, repair, and possible resale. Recently, I was reminded of repair when I paid $60 to have the poles of my beloved three-man tent restrung. The inner elastic cordage went limp earlier than expected after four summers of use and storage. The purchase of a new tent was tempting. I could justify it by citing upgraded designs over the years with advanced engineering. But they also came with the buy-once-cry-once sticker price of $300-$500. My renewed pole segments eagerly snap together, and my love for the tent has been re-invigorated.

No gear list is definitive. Equipment collections are personal and customized to be as unique as each individual and destination. Your inventory may require additions or justify subtractions from mine, but remember, these few items have made the cut after thousands of miles. Each has earned a spot, deemed worthy-to-pack, valued as worth-their-weight, and missed if forgotten. Use the following real-world insights to deliberate your next purchases, avoid waste, and glean hard-won lessons.

Last Thoughts on The Big Three

Although we assessed some considerations for sleeping systems, tents, packs, and footwear in previous chapters, a few final notes need addressing.

Packs offered in lighter-weight options have the least structure. You won't find a traditional suspension system spreading the load evenly around your back and into your hip belt as there's hardly a *load* to spread when packing light. Aluminum external frames evolved into plastic-sheet internal planks decades ago. Then internal frames became unneeded with ever-decreasing base weights. These minimal packs are lidless, roll-top, have few pockets, are two pounds or less, and sport little-to-no back or hip padding. For example, my current pack has less structure than my teenager's school backpack. It carries 50 liters, weighs 18 ounces, and has no padding nor frame against my back. It has a minimally padded hip belt, no lid, a few exterior stretch pockets, and ample external straps.

Are you concerned about comfort? Don't be.

Ensuring hard items aren't stuffed against the spine will prevent friction rubs. As a backup, slide a small closed-cell foam butt pad along the inner chamber for a makeshift back cushion. Even when toting an early-trip maxed-out load in the mid-twenties (after food and water), the pack is perfectly comfortable. Don't be afraid of these paradigm-busting minimal models.

The principle is the less you carry, the less structure is needed to bear the load. And as pack structure is reduced, so follows pack weight, further lightening your total weight.

Sleeping bag fills, compression, and strategies have been described previously. Remember that mummy bags are cut narrow, especially from the hips downward. Some brands are cut slimmer than others as a sneaky weight-saving body-warming strategy. Others save weight with zippers that end at the hip. Warmth efficiency is improved with the tighter cut, just like a well-fitted jacket, but it's restricting all night. Buyers tend to look at length but should be comparing shoulder- and hip-width measurements instead before purchase. Not all mummy bags are the same shape. Broad-shouldered or full-figured hikers should be vigilant about these more telling, horizontal-comfort measurements. This slender style also limits how your hand can operate the zipper. Confusing counsel abounds about whether to select a right- or left-zip bag. It may seem logical to recommend a right-zipping bag to a right-hander, but the opposite is true in a real-world setting, especially in snug down. Reaching diagonally across your belly to operate a zipper near the opposite hip and moving it up to your ear with your dominant hand provides greater mobility than attempting this on the same side. In other words, right-handers should seek left-zip bags. Operating the opposite-side zipper avoids awkwardly straining your wrist and cramming your dominant elbow into your gut to run the zipper. For you 10-percenters out there with a strong left hand, select right-zip bags.

Tent fabric, like sleeping bag fill, can be compressed on the trail but needs to relax off-season. Make sure you're allowing both a generous bag during long-term storage.

Don't be afraid to uninvite the retail stuff sack provided with your tent. They are designed to host both poles and fabric. That's great for car camping but impractical when space is at a premium in smaller packs. Separate poles from fabric. Make the poles ride on pack exteriors. They pair nicely next to a rigid fly rod case. Then take the remaining fabric (body, fly, and tarp) and see how compact they can smash into a smaller stuff sack. Use a compression sack for a slightly heavier-but-satisfying option if you want to crank it down. If you're curious, I've done the research for you: a 10-liter compression sack is two ounces more than a one-ounce drawstring sack of the same size.

Inflatable pillows are a strategic part of sleep systems yet dismissed as optional or luxury. Mine is 3.8 ounces and worthy of permanence. Various models are far superior to the classic pillow-creation approach of jamming a jacket in a stuff sack or balling up additional clothing, not that this doesn't work, but it's lumpy and inconsistent. Use it to get by in the rare case you find yourself mid-trip with a hole in your pillow.

Inflatables use a bladder inside a fabric case. Look for something lined with microfiber or soft fleece. If not, you can also stuff it inside a shirt. If you lay it slick side down, it will drive you crazy as it slides around on your pad or tent floor. Softer fabric grips it into place and softens it against your face. The one downside is if they're over-inflated, it can feel like balancing your head on a balloon. Using less air equals more contour. Don't max them out, or a neck strain awaits you in the morning.

Pro tip: stuff your deflated pillow in with your sleeping bag before your cinch the stuff sack drawstring.

Essential Apparel

Clothing is weighed like other gear but ultimately divided into two categories: worn or carried. The carried items count toward your pack's base weight. Hiking footwear will never be on your back but is still an important piece to weigh to prevent the often-overlooked thigh fatigue they cause if over-built.

Hiking pants constructed with ripstop nylon or lightweight polyester blends offer a quick dry and durability. Desirable features include cargo pockets, bugproof weaves, gusseted knees for ease of movement, and a few zippered pockets for safety. Some are categorized as convertible to shorts as leg pants get unzipped on warm days. I've abandoned interest in zip-off legs for three reasons.

One, as much as we'd all rather be in shorts during summer days, it requires managing more mosquito spray. Every inch of skin covered with cool, bugproof clothing equals fewer ounces of picaridin you'll need to pack. If you find yourself too warm—a rarity at altitude—layer down your top, scrunch long-sleeves up the arms, or wet a hat or gaiter for a chilling swamp-cooler effect. The chilling rush of icy spring water dripping off your hat behind your ears will dash your desires for shorts.

Reason two, shorts are slick for maintained trails, but anglers are off the trail enough to prefer the shin protection needed to bushwhack riparian vegetation that guards alpine streams. Lastly, the cross-thigh convertible zipper is bulky and rubs upper thighs and kneecaps after miles of marching. Straight leg fabric is preferred as it provides ease of motion and flexibility.

To combat the heat generated from pumping thighs, hiking pants offer mesh front pockets to work as hidden crotch vents. Take circulation a step further with an unorthodox method that keeps thighs and groins cool while wearing pants—keep your fly unzipped. When I confess to hiking companions that I walk this way, they are shocked.

My retort, "Who's going to care?"

Seldomly have I chatted with oncoming traffic and had them notice. Most of the time, they don't—or don't dare to say anything. When and if they *do* point it out, I shrug and say, "I know. I like it that way."

A free-range fly offers direct air conditioning in a headwind, significantly lower temperatures all day long, reduced chaffing, and is a symbolic reminder of your solitude. An untucked shirt offers a portion of privacy not to offend others along the trail. The only downside is forgetting to zip before group photos. Far too many of my best pics have been marred with an open fly.

Whatever the model, choose wisely. Your pants will be your primary bottom half the entire journey. The lower legs may get muddy on hiking days, then rinsed clean each river ford. Don't sweat it if a few spots of pine pitch stain the rear or a small tear starts on a back pocket from hopping large talus. That's part of the adventure.

A **lightweight base layer** is your second pair of pants. Long Johns, leggings, athletic pants, compression pants— they come in many names. Primarily used at night or layered with hiking pants during cold weather, they offer stretchy, compression comfort and variety. They aren't much for mosquito-proofing unless made with a tight compression weave. Ladies will want a quality pair with a tight weave if wearing leggings as their primary hiking pant. Close-woven material will reduce continual repellent application. For guys using them for layering and sleeping, select a thin, lightweight fabric as they also come in medium- and heavy-weights for cold weather.

Consider sleeping in them for three reasons. One, they increase the temperature rating of your bag, allowing you to carry lighter-weight down. Second, they reduce body oil build-up on the interior bag lining. Base layers extend the life of the bag fabric, decrease grime, and are easier to launder than down bags. Third, they keep thighs from sticking together while sleeping. It's impractical to bathe daily in the backcountry. A quick wet-handkerchief wipe-down before bed reduces oily thighs but having a thin layer of clothing between legs can increase comfort.

When you awake to whipping wind or a quick squall of summer snow, keep them on your legs under hiking pants until afternoon. The layered combination can't be beat.

Rain pants can additionally protect if the weather gets endlessly wet or winterlike. The three layers combined can endure temperatures in the teens. But I don't always bring rain pants. Checking the forecast can help you gauge the need to carry the weight and bulk of this item. It's optional on my list unless I see a cold front settling in or headed into the Pacific Northwest. Otherwise, quick-moving warm-weather rainstorms are tolerable wearing nylon pants combined with a quality rain jacket and a cheap plastic poncho. Hiking pants can absorb and diffuse most rain without risking hypothermia as quickly as a soaked upper body.

Hooded rain jackets are a must-carry. They aren't just for rain as they are excellent windbreakers and the ultimate bug barrier. Most of the use of your rain jacket will be for wind and bugs. Ironic as it may seem, when it's raining, avoid standing around to test materials. Unless in hot pursuit of a rising trout, duck for cover with the jacket to moderate moisture permeation.

Modern fabrics are advancing each year with promises of enhanced breathability and lasting waterproofness. However, users agree they're much better at the latter, as even the best materials struggle to breathe out warm, moist body heat through wetted fabric. Don't plan on hiking miles in the rain without fogging up the insides of your sleeves with warm moisture. The breathability works while holding still, but not for extended activity. Some models offer pit zips to address ventilation, but zipper-laden jackets increase their weight. Look for more minimal designs. Selecting bold colors can add safety and easier identification of who's who around a camp.

While we're on color, seize chances to purchase a variety

of colors. Don't default to black or gray for everything. It's not a fashion contest out there. There is a sensible benefit to having each item intentionally *not* match. The advantage comes when fumbling around in your pack's interior rifling for the cobalt blue neck gaiter, the lime green hiking shirt, the bold red rain jacket, or the tan base layer. Black is a popular outerwear color, but when everything is black, and it's dark in your tent, you'll get annoyed finding your black microfleece beanie.

Warm jackets, like sleeping bags, are filled with sophisticated synthetic batting or goose down. Some brands even chemically coated their proprietary down to shore up its natural waterproof weakness. Fleece jackets are acceptable but can be the single heaviest item in your apparel. Some enjoy having their down jacket be hooded, similar to their rain jacket. I'm not of that camp. If I'm *that* cold, I keep my skull warm under a fleece beanie and neck gaiter and spare the added few ounces, bulk, and cost a hood adds to an already-pricey jacket.

Combining a warm poly or down jacket under a hooded rain jacket is a surefire combination to combat low temps. Durability aside, the combo could be warm enough for winter sledding or alpine skiing. Cozy jackets can cut the chill all evening and morning. They can even be slept in or hiked in if needed when temperatures drop. Similar to rain jackets, optional zippered pockets in the chest or bicep increase weight. Look for sleek designs from a reputable brand that offers a warranty for low cost-per-wear and long life. It will be one of your more expensive investments, but worth it for years.

Long-sleeve hiking shirt selection isn't easy. As a fundamental staple, it's used almost as much as your hiking pants. Retailers have a variety of options, but most are essentially running shirts. Backpacking is also sweaty athletic travel. The shirt needs between the two sports are near-identical, but running shirts are ubiquitous, offering more choices at lower prices.

There are trade-offs to consider with your next top. Fancy hiking and running shirts offer meshy pits and spines for ventilation, but this opens you up to—you guessed it—more bug spray. Vented fabric sections are so comfortable in warm weather or for the sweaty among us, but a risk. The Catch-22 is the more breathable the fabric, the more a mosquito can pierce through it, whereas tighter weaves repel bugs but deplete airflow and suffocate sweat glands.

Quarter-zip tops offer a generous chest sweat vent. Popping up the collar cuts down on neck sunburns, even if just an inch or two more than a crew neck. Another strike against typical crew necks—the front yokes become an irritant as they ride up into the throat under the backward-leaning weight of shoulder straps. Anything button-down or zippered will prevent this bother and better vent your chest heat. Shirts with thumbholes are ideal for the long-armed or a cozy cool-day option.

But what about when it's hot?

Similar to the dismissal of removable pant legs or shorts, I stopped carrying short-sleeve shirts years ago unless I'm diving into deep arid canyons to explore big rivers. When it's too hot for long-sleeves, bottom-out a chest zipper and scrunch up the sleeves on forearms. I've yet to find a flawless hiking top that's both breathable and bugproof, so I lean toward the prior and add some spray to my triceps and shoulders where fabric is flush and most vulnerable.

Button-down nylon shirts come close to the balance of the two bugproof-versus-breathable demands, but don't stretch and move like athletic tops. These shirts are built for anglers and may not provide interest for the average backpacker, equipped with Velcro chest pockets, button-down collars, back vents, and a bugproof weave. You can hike distances in them if needed when a hiking shirt is a tad too chilly, too bitten, or too smelly days later. Fly boxes and other fishing tools slide into the chest pockets removing the need to carry a hip pack.

When arriving at a campsite, before setting up a tent or start nesting any gear, one of the first things to do is dangle your sweaty hiking shirt from a tree and don this more day-hike-handy utility shirt instead. Depending on its severity, the hiking shirt might get dunked in the drink before the sun goes down for a fresher tomorrow.

A **long-sleeved sleeping shirt** is the third top carried. More commonly known as a cool-weather top or base layer, not everyone calls it a sleeping shirt. It serves more of a purpose than sleep, but that's its primary use for me. There's no need for lake-laundering this cozy layer. It's rarely used for hiking. I wear it all night with my sexy stretchy tights as I sleep cold. But around camp, it's the perfect close-fitting could-be-compression base layer under a down or rain jacket. Similar to hiking shirts, you may find utility in quarter-zip collars more so than simple crew collars. Thumbholes are helpful too.

These five layers—two jackets and three shirts—are the entirety of what you'll need in the alpine. If not angling, drop the fishing shirt. If hot weather is guaranteed, add a t-shirt. That's it. All should be quick-drying and cotton-free. Each has a stand-alone purpose plus can be paired for added warmth or utility with another, depending on conditions. Don't be tempted to add additional shirts. Instead, do laundry or come home slightly stinky. More does not equal better—only more ounces and bulk.

Apparel Accessories

Wool socks are the undisputed champions of blister prevention as they wick moisture and manage heat. Rather than high-octane wool, smart hiking socks are partially woven with other synthetics to blend additional benefits of cost, weight, comfort, and stretch. Look for mostly wool blends that mix polyester, nylon, or spandex. Don't feel compelled to get expensive brands. For years, I hiked comfortably in club warehouse hiking socks at a fraction of the cost. Name-brand socks will have more advanced stitching when you're ready for the upgrade.

If going the one-shoe, hike-wet route introduced in Chapter Six, use a thinner quick-drying sock. Slim socks will accelerate dry time after a ford as your shoe is draining. In fact, choose a lighter-weight sock regardless. Placed in a warm, waterproof boot, this will decrease blister-causing heat. There's no need for anything more than light- or medium-weight until shoulder seasons. If you're sweaty, go with a lightweight sock and switch regularly.

Crew tops pair nicely with long pants, protect against a little mud, but don't protect against mosquitos. You'll still need to spray your ankles above your boots in camp. Shorter tops are practical when hiking in shorts. I recommend carrying three pairs. Rotate between two along the trail—one wet and one dry. One set is regularly catching rays as it dangles well-secured from the drying rack, otherwise known as the top of your pack. The third pair lives in the bottom of the bag to keep toes cozy (and bag clean) at night. Similar to alternate shirts, feel free on the last day to bury the beat-up trail socks and hike out in your sleeping socks for that fresh feeling during your final miles.

On that note, stash a change of clothes and a stick of deodorant in the car for the drive home. This wardrobe makeover will keep you from being mistaken for the homeless when you're ordering a heavy celebration meal at a restaurant.

A **neck gaiter** is a recent addition to the list. After rolling my eyes at them for years, thinking they looked silly or overly bandit-like, I gave one a try. Permanent residency was immediately granted. They are the real deal. Dipped in a creek and left limp around a neck, they prevent the pain from scorched skin and ear burns. Kept dry among bugs, they reduce the need for annoying face spray. Stretched over the back of the skull, they add evening warmth to a beanie. Rumor has it you can wear them as a headband, but I haven't attempted that fashion statement quite yet.

A **fleece beanie** is essential. Some use a polyester or woven wool beanie, but microfleece is my lightweight go-to. Anything that serves the purpose of warming the back of your ears and neck will work.

A **brimmed hat or ball cap** is also critical. Keep the sun off your face and the blinding burn of midday off your brow. Full-brimmed hats are popular, whether with flexible fabric or rigid western wear. I prefer the packability of stuffing a floppy fabric cap into an exterior pack pocket. If the sun is scorching, my ears and neck get protected with a neck gaiter or handkerchief.

Underwear style is a personal decision. I carry two pairs and rotate washing and wearing, similar to socks. Select synthetics, never cotton blends, and look for breathable or mesh features. Dark colors are prudent for reasons I'll let you guess.

Handkerchief color is up to you. Their purpose is covered on pages 28 and 107. Choose a bold color for flare and personal style. No other multiple-use item has such endless utility.

Small Gear Stuffed in a Pouch

Smartphones have become the primary digital camera for most of the world—and rightfully so. They're remarkable, thin, and more waterproof each year. Tucked in a front pocket on airplane mode, they're handy to catch that perfect moment or wildlife encounter. Face it inward while stowed in a pocket for added impact protection. They're great for online mapping, note-taking, and e-books, but watch your battery life. If on airplane mode during the day and turned off overnight, it can last all week without a charge, even with reasonable camera use.

A **charging pack** looks like a large tube of lipstick. This device gives you peace of mind that you won't run powerless midweek, but on the heavier side for such a small widget, weighing three to four ounces. Shop for the more compact and less powerful options as they will be the lightest weight. Don't buy ultra-powerful models. Knowing your phone's battery capacity (e.g., 2,800 or 3,900 mAH) can help you select an associated charging capability. Amazon has a good selection.

Don't forget a short **charging cable**, or the charging pack is worthless. Rather than tangling with universal three-foot cables, inches-long cables are also available online.

Headlamp choices on the market are endless. Each year they get lighter, brighter, and more battery efficient. I buy a new one regularly as last year's model goes on sale, each more lightweight than the previous. You can't have enough lying around the house, the toolbox, or the car. It takes several seasons to burn out two lithium AAA batteries, but carry spares, nonetheless. Look for models that require two batteries instead of three. It makes life easy and efficient as batteries are sold in four-packs. Also, look for smooth-dimming features and a red-light option. Use both features to avoid blinding your buddy and burning up the battery. It's rare to need them on full blast.

Lifehack: when night hiking, don't wear them on your head. Sure, it's more convenient, but holding it like a flashlight in your hand casts longer shadows exposing each trail bump and dip. You'll stumble far less as contours gain depth in lower-held light.

The **two extra batteries** may not be used this outing, but patience, my friend, all in due time. When you least expect it, you'll be glad you have them. Using lithium rather than alkaline is worth every extra penny. They are shockingly light and long-lasting.

Topographic maps are the treasure hunt in your pocket. As discussed in Chapter Five, learning to read them is essential for safety, orientation, trip success, and route alterations. Carrying entire quadrangle maps or range-wide, folded, waterproof maps can be excessive and clumsy. Instead, use online printing options to generate dialed-in custom sections. Print them in color on high-quality, high-gloss cover paper for a touch of weatherproofing. Truly waterproof paper is pricey. If it's going to be that wet, throw them in a sandwich baggie. Let them ride folded in a cargo pocket for quick access and on-the-go reference. Save a pic on your phone as a backup.

There's an old-school romance to unfolding a paper topographic map while catching your breath along the trail. Advanced subscription-based mapping apps make slick substitutions while viewed on GPS-aware smartphones. But paper commands no battery power nor satellite signal.

First-aid kits always feel inadequate when solo. There's a looming sense of "will it be enough." But reality settles the mind when you remember that wilderness first aid, whether self-administered or provided, by its very nature and definition, will always be somewhat inadequate, hence the name *first* aid. You can only carry so much. When it's time to treat, combining kits with those in a group or borrowed from other campers adds to a communal effort if a situation is dire. Pre-made sensible kits weigh only a few ounces. Butterfly closures (like Steri-Strips) are a savvy addition.

Medicine needs will vary from person to person. As explained on page 155, carry ibuprofen and an anti-diarrheal at minimum. Some prefer generics of Advil PM or Tylenol PM that not only cut down on the day's sore spots but add a sleep aid. I'm a morning person and dislike the grogginess they can cause. Others may consider an antihistamine, depending on the season. Small trial-size containers reduce bulk.

Mosquito repellent is addressed on page 141. To second the challenge previously introduced, try other-than-DEET products. Try it for the better smell. Stay for the equivalent repellent ability.

Water treatment drops (page 108)

Mini lighters are located at gas stations easier than grocery stores. Choose a bright color.

Waterproof matches are your backup fire starter.

Duct tape fits when wrapped around said lighter but prevents you from seeing the remaining gas level. Compact mini rolls are sold in camping aisles.

A **knife** should be foldable, minimal, and sharp enough to gut a fish. Heavy metal handles are unnecessary. Search for sturdy plastic handles to cut weight. Mine has a built-in whistle.

Whistles are commonly being built right into the chest strap buckle of packs, right below your chin. If not, add a plastic one.

Urethane glue is a trip-saver. Speaking from specific experiences, a tiny tube provides enough to repair a leaky inflatable pad, a flopping boot tread, a stick-torn tent vestibule, and a pack exterior puncture if left to set overnight. Combine with duct tape, and you'll make it work.

Disposable poncho (page 60)

A gear-on-the-floor shakedown can help sort out what's critical.

Kitchen garbage bags are similar to the cotton handkerchief—you can't tally the miscellaneous uses. Waterproof solutions include snowfield glissade sled, downpour pack cover, sub-par poncho, sleeping bag stuff-sack enhancement, smellables guard inside a food bag, kitchen tablecloth, and of course, a trash bag for when you encounter litter.

Kitchenware

Stoves are light-years ahead of where they were decades ago. A few commercial options collapse together inside cylindrical pots like nesting dolls. They're gas-efficient and ultra-handy. Boiling water is ready before you've unpackaged your food. For the do-it-yourselfer, several lightweight homemade models are shared online using liquid fuel or powered by stick fire.

Fuel is sold separately. Canisters of isobutane-propane mix are the most common. Don't be confused by feeling the need to match your stove brand and fuel. They're interchangeable, like various gasoline brands. DIY stoves use liquid white gas.

A **silicone or plastic mug** is desirable for steamy beef stroganoff during dinner and cinnamon oatmeal in the morning. And that may not even be required if eating out of the pouch or out of quart-sized freezer baggies. Boiling water can soak pasta or oatmeal and will not warp freezer bags. You'll want to use your hat as an oven mitt to hold them.

Long-handled sporks are the only utensil needed for pouch meals. And I've gone entire weeks without this tool. A well-carved stick can act as a mini spade to scoop pasta into your mouth. Two smooth twigs equal chopsticks. Innovate, adapt, overcome! Short-handled sporks are annoying. When eating freeze-dried meals, your hand gets stamped with sticky sauce reaching for the last bite. If stirring condiments into chunk light tuna for a no-cook wrap, the bottom chunks of meat are out of reach.

Foil for baking trout is carried by the confident angler, certain of their abilities. See page 155 for more.

Filters are studied on pages 107-108.

Hydration bladders and their handy hoses are the way to go. Ditch the hard plastic bottles. Bladders are half the weight, twice the capacity, slide into any pocket, shrink while you drink, and their hanging hoses remind you to drink more often. Hard bottles are awkward to remove and return to your pack's side holsters. If you're going to use a bottle, buy a 1-liter from the bottled water aisle of a grocery store with a push-pull drinking cap.

A **bear rope** and a **small carabiner** can heft your food bag into a tree. It doesn't need to be a heavy-duty rope. Fifty feet of nylon utility cord is ideal. Black bears are incredible climbers, so keep it away from the trunk. Grizzlies stand taller than you think, so shoot for basketball hoop height. Squirrels are a likely threat. If the perfect tree branch isn't in sight or you feel a tall bear could reach your bag, still hang it. Something is better than nothing. Better off the ground for innovative critters and bears more focused on crumbs.

Toiletries

Toothbrushes don't need to be cut in half—an absurd ultralight tactic. Travel brushes are handy as they collapse together or carried without the case. One hack: add a dot of toothpaste to the inside of the travel toothbrush case. Better yet, compact disposable mini toothbrushes are also practical, have a built-in toothpick, and include minty dots for toothpaste.

Floss is my primary tooth care. Between flossing, chewing gum daily, and brushing my teeth with a tiny disposable toothbrush, I must confess, I stopped carrying toothpaste.

Gum is amazing. I may have an addiction.

Contact case and a mini solution dropper may be on your list.

Mini plastic one-ounce bottles are translucent and sold at outdoor retailers. Fill one with a mild **hair and body wash,** one with **baby powder** for chaffing, and one with **sunblock.** Less-than-one-ounce bottles are event better.

Lotion is a luxury I carry for hammered hands and cheeks. Travel-size tubes are available in grocery stores.

Earplugs may change how you sleep as the mind races at night, especially when solo. Evening winds roar through the trees. Nocturnal rodents and gangly ungulates rustle right through camp. All of them sound like a 500-pound grizzly— not that I know exactly how that sounds. But if one visits, I'm okay snoozing through. If she wants to talk, she'll wake me up. Like an untrusting cowboy sleeping with one hand on his pistol, my bear spray canister is within arms-reach. It can't go in my tent for fear of accidental discharge, but it's upright in an open shoe "holster" ready for quick-draw deployment.

Lip balm isn't just for lips; it's helpful for haggard fingertips after navigating the sandpaper handholds of granite talus. It's pleasant for nostril bottoms after a windy day of dripping snot. I've even used it—shh—for relieving a chafed groin.

Toilet paper for camping comes in tight rolls. It's marketed to be more biodegradable, and I hope that's the case, but I have my doubts. I've never circled back to check the following year. Bury it deep and stir in the dirt with a stick to give it a decomposition head start. More cathole strategies are sheepishly reviewed on pages 132-134.

Wipes are marketed to be biodegradable or septic-tank-friendly. Again, be skeptical of the claim. Wipes are more practical to carry back to camp and bury in your kitchen trash bag than toilet paper. One less piece of litter in (or under) the wilderness is worth it. Tossing used wipes in a fire is an instant solution.

Nail clippers are for quiet and calm times. You've had a swim. You're feeling clean. Maybe you've flossed or smeared lotion—time to feel especially civilized and clip your nasty nails.

Extras

Optional and luxury items include sunglasses, a deck of cards, gaiters, a small book, a journal, a flask, and a camera, among other things that might help your comfort and enjoyment. You're on vacation—act like it!

Camp/creek shoes pair with traditional waterproof boots, unless hiking wet in breathable-mesh low tops. (See pages 90-92)

Trekking poles are popular but not mandatory. They're ideal for spreading demand and fatigue beyond leg power by engaging arm muscles. The benefit comes when biceps and triceps alleviate quads from bearing the entire burden of a steep climb, softening a jarring descent, or stabilizing a stream ford. The con: they don't add much on mild grades. Worse, they interrupt your intuitive gait if your gaze is centered on perpetual pole-tip placement. On maintained straightaways, bushwhacking through heavy timber, or mild downgrades on trails, they're more hassle than help. If you're minding your knees and joints and would like to spread the wear-and-tear, give them a try. If you're interested in keeping it simple, skip them.

Light gloves fall in the same category—useful but not mandatory. They alleviate scarred palms and fingertips when the route shows several scrambles up steep sections of talus or scree. They also help cold hands during frosty mornings. The only con is managing the clutter and weight associated with an item that may only find a use for an hour or two the entire week.

Anna warms up in the setting sun with her one luxury item—a small book.

Butt pad—sorry—*sitting* pad is more appropriate. The ground is cold and hard. Make it warm and soft with a seat-size piece of closed-cell foam. Commercial offerings run $10-15 and mere one or two ounces. Custom-cut your own from an old blue foam pad and slide it against your back for dual uses.

Headphones are a tad controversial. Debates linger about their ethic along the trail. I carried them early on to help tune out miles and get the pump in my pace while marching to the rhythm. The downside of using headphones is you miss out on precious silence—something civilized society stamps out. Silence is golden.

Additionally, open ears are a safety mechanism. Allow your senses to detect dangers like the startled moose crashing through the brush or a falling branch. Hearing the echoing elk bugle or eagle call is a treat. Keep your antennae up while on the move. Heaven forbid a stranded or injured hiker is yelling or using a whistle to grab your attention while you stroll by bouncing to a beat.

If you crave music to color your world, save it for times of safety and solitude, in a tent or the peak. Playlists have alleviated misery while sitting out prolonged storms and have nearly brought me to tears while pondering on a vista.

Bear spray isn't always carried. Only you can make that call if the 11 ounces are worth their weight after studying your area's likelihood of an encounter.

It's anecdotal, and I hesitate to share this as I don't want to direct your decision, but as many times as I've wandered deep into bear country—even grizzly country—I've yet to encounter a backcountry bear. (Knock on wood.)

Every bear I've witnessed has been casually eating along the busy roads and popular day-hiking trails within the boundaries of Grand Teton and Yellowstone National Parks.

On some outings, I long to spot one—at a safe distance, of course—to get over with it. On others, I wipe my brow when I return to the car after stepping over scat piles all week.

I want to think my streak results from diligence at prevention by making noise, whistling, chatting, and even singing along the trail. I'm also vigilant about hanging my food. But bear populations are growing annually in every state. They can't avoid me forever. Something tells me that when I finally see one, it will be on a trip I didn't carry spray.

Fly-Fishing Gear

The Bible of backcountry angling has been canonized by Rich Osthoff in *Fly-Fishing the Rocky Mountain Backcountry*. Far be it for me to attempt to add to the decades of doctrine shared in this comprehensive guidebook. Included instead is a short packing list and a few tips for fellow backcountry anglers.

I have an unproven theory that 95% of fishing is done within eyesight of a parked car. That number may be higher. Hiking a mere 15 minutes, about one mile, separates your approach from the crowds. A short hike places you in territory less trodden. More importantly, walking engages you with trout that rarely see artificial flies.

Rod cases are obscenely heavy, especially the airline-grade aluminum ones sold with high-end rods. A quick hack to save weight is purchased at your local home improvement store. Buy a plastic fluorescent light bulb cover. Cut to length. Adhere one end as the bottom. Leave the other cap as the top. Don't slide your four-piece segments in without some fabric sleeve or the eyelets will scratch the rod while hiking. A handkerchief, at minimum, will do and also serves as a spare hand towel.

Fly rod needs in backcountry water can vary. 6-weight rods can punch a bead-head wooly bugger through headwinds and battle a bruiser if you connect with one but overpowered for small trout. 4-weight rods can best skeeter an elk hair caddis for opportunistic trout on pocket-water streams, but struggle when long-range firepower is needed to reach faraway rise forms. The balance between the two is the 5-weight. It has the punch to target cruising trout, and the light touch for stream strategies. 4-piece fly rods are great but when you're tired of the case catching on low-hanging branches as it stands high above your pack height, spoil yourself with a six-piece travel rod.

Fly reel. Don't forget it. Treat yourself to a fresh tapered leader the night before takeoff.

Licenses can be obtained online and printed at home to save the hassle of an extra stop after crossing state lines. Follow the policy and make this purchase. It's easy to justify that your chances of being checked are low when 15 miles into a wilderness area, but it's the law. Being caught without incurs steep penalties to save a few bucks. Furthermore, permit fees are spent on conservation to enhance fishing's future.

Foam fly cases are a lightweight angler's friend. Hard-backed cases can get bulky and weighty. Minimize your selection down to two or three pocket-sized boxes. They should slide into cargo pant pockets, chest pockets, or jacket hand pockets. Close the zippers on these pockets to avoid heartbreak. There's no need to tote an additional hip pack if keeping your inventory simple.

If you favor additional room for water and a rain jacket for longer days exploring shorelines and streams, use your emptied backpack. Dump it out in your tent and load it with the day's water, food, raingear, and fishing needs. Some internal-frame models offer a removable plastic stay for an instant daypack imitation. Packs shrink to half the size when compression straps are pulled tight, creating a slender daypack-sized setup for smaller needs.

Critical flies are wooly buggers, scuds, eggs, mayflies, caddisflies, small stoneflies, and a selection of terrestrials like hoppers, beetles, and large ants. Deep in the high alpine, where frigid gin-clear lakes shine deep and tumbling streams provide holding water, thousands of trout rarely see an artificial fly all summer. You can fool 90% of them with a #10 bead-head black wooly bugger, a #12 olive scud, a #8 orange scud, a #14 elk hair caddis, or a #16 parachute Adams. A more expansive arsenal is wise but bring plenty of these sure-fire staples. Stealth, timing, position, and presentation far outweigh perfect fly selection.

Tapered leader spares are needed after windy days and maddening fly-switching among finicky eaters. A three-pack is plenty for a week.

Polarized sunglasses under a brimmed hat are the difference-maker between fishing blind and having near x-ray vision. In these crystal-clear waters under wide-open skies, trout are experts at spotting you. Even the playing field.

A **lanyard** is another tool to reduce the need for a hip pack. Include 4x- and 5x-**tippet spools**. There's rarely a need for 6x in the backcountry. Fish can be tippet-savvy, but this isn't tailwater trickery. Also included are **fly floatant**, a **hemostat**, and **nippers**.

Your reel, lanyard, and fly boxes can fit into an unused stuff sack. At the bottom of the bag, toss in a few **indicators** and **BB-sized weights** for nymphing.

A net isn't listed as I stopped packing one. Learning to beach or tail-grip a big trout enhances gear simplicity.

As you refine your fishing gear down to these mandatory few items, you'll better enjoy the freedom of movement required to be angling in the alpine. Pure streams and pristine lakes await to assess your skills. The fluorescent stripes and spots of wild trout that swim at altitude await your best presentation. You'll likely be the first angler they've ever met. I love examining each species before release.

The following poetic passage by Rich Osthoff sums up the experience and is worth rehearsing aloud at trailheads before embarking on any trek targeting elusive golden trout.

"I love just roaming the mountains, but it's the thrill of catching big trout in improbable lakes among the peaks that lures me back so religiously. And the allure of trophy golden trout is the strongest of all. When you get right down to it, you can catch every other trout that swims in the high country at sea level as well. But to pursue goldens, you have to travel high into their rarefied realm of enveloping clouds, booming thunder, and dazzling light. Cradled briefly in disbelieving hands, a big, radiant golden is a fitting culmination to such a journey."

Made in United States
North Haven, CT
15 July 2022